# Pilgrimage into Pentecost

# Pilgrimage into Pentecost
## *The Pneumatological Legacy of*
# *Howard M. Ervin*

### BY DANIEL D. ISGRIGG
With a Foreword by William W. Menzies

**Word & Spirit Press**
Tulsa, Oklahoma

Copyright © 2008 by Daniel D. Isgrigg

http://danieldisgrigg.blogspot.com

All rights reserved. Written permission must be secured from the publisher to use or reproduce any part of this book except for brief quotations in critical reviews or articles. Printed in the United States of America

Published in Tulsa, Oklahoma, by Word & Spirit Press

WordSP@gmail.com
http://WandSP.com

Book design and composition by Bob Bubnis / Booksetters, Bowling Green, Kentucky

Cover photograph of Howard M. Ervin © Oral Roberts University. Used by permission and with gratitude.

ISBN 10: 0-9785352-7-8

ISBN 13: 978-0-9785352-7-8

∞ The paper used in this publication meets the minimum requirements of the American National Standard for Information Sciences—Permanence of Paper for Printed Library Materials, ANSI Z39.48-1992.

Unless otherwise indicated, Scripture quotations are from the HOLY BIBLE, NEW INTERNATIONAL VERSION, © 1973, 1978, 1984 by International Bible Society. Used by permission of Zondervan Publishing House. All rights reserved.

# Foreword

In *Pilgrimage into Pentecost,* Daniel D. Isgrigg provides serious students of Pentecostalism two useful services. First, he gives the reader an interesting and detailed accounting of the life of Howard M. Ervin; and second, he outlines the main contours of Ervin's theology of the Holy Spirit.

The study follows the journey of Baptist preacher/theologian Ervin from his early days as an agnostic through his encounter with God. It traces Ervin's early pastoral days, and follows him on to his embracing of the Pentecostal message and experience. Isgrigg follows the long tenure of Ervin as a theology faculty member at Oral Roberts University into his current life of retirement. *Pilgrimage* then points out Ervin's strong exegetical and theological defense of the classical Pentecostal message of Baptism in the Holy Spirit, as well as his loyalty to his American Baptist roots. The work shows how Ervin engaged in a spirited defense of his theology against a variety of critics and how the unity of the Spirit among Christians was foremost in Ervin's desires. Isgrigg makes a strong case for the ecumenical ministry of Ervin over the years.

*Pilgrimage into Pentecost* highlights several key features of Ervin's theology: Ervin argues persuasively for the "birthday of the Church" being in John 20, not Acts 2. He anchors his belief in evidential tongues for Spirit baptism in the models provided in the Book of Acts; and he departs from most Pentecostal scholars in his advocacy of "one Baptism; one filling." In each of these issues, the author documents Ervin's line of argumentation copiously.

It was more than 40 years ago, when I was a young student of Pentecostalism, that I first encountered the writings of Howard M. Ervin. His persuasive apologetic for classical Pentecostal theology, even though he was a Charismatic Baptist, powerfully encouraged me. I have noted with pleasure the long years of faithful ministry and writing of Ervin, one who has not altered his views from his early days. He has been a strong advocate against those who would weaken the belief that God has wanted to empower His people for evangelism and missions with the empowerment of the Spirit in a crisis experience of Spirit baptism, accompanied by the sign of speaking in tongues.

In *Pilgrimage into Pentecost*, Daniel Isgrigg provides Pentecostals and Charismatics—and all interested in this burgeoning international movement of the Spirit—with a well-deserved study of the life and thought of one of its pioneers. Through this work, many can be grateful for the pioneering scholarly ministry of Dr. Ervin and understand his distinctive contribution.

> — William W. Menzies
> President Emeritus and Chancellor,
> Asia Pacific Theological Seminary
> Author, *Anointed to Serve: The Story of the Assemblies of God*
> February 2008
> Springfield, Missouri

# Acknowledgments

I would like to thank my wife, Amonda, for supporting me in all the areas of my life. She has supported me through my education and is the reason I was able to complete this manuscript. Thanks for being my biggest fan. I would like to recognize Dr. Cheryl Iverson of Oral Roberts University for her suggestion to pursue this project and her encouragement to publish this material. I want to thank Dr. Mark E. Roberts of Word and Spirit Press. Dr. Roberts has been a loyal friend and colleague in addition to being an encouraging publisher. Thank you for the opportunity to get this information into the hands of the next generation. I would also like to thank my friend, mentor, and pastor, Dr. Gregory L. Davis of Christian Chapel in Tulsa. Thank you for helping me find and do God's will for my life.

Finally, I would like to thank the subject of this book, Dr. Howard M. Ervin. Dr. Ervin has graciously made himself available to me for my research. He willingly accommodated my interviews even after his retirement and allowed the content of his life to be open to this project. The opportunities I had to visit with Dr. Ervin will be cherished. His legacy of scholarship, commitment to Christ, and his teaching on pneumatology has been the inspiration for this book, and I pray it will bring honor to him and his legacy.

# Contents

Foreword by William W. Menzies . . . . . . . . . . . . . . . . . .5

Acknowledgments . . . . . . . . . . . . . . . . . . . . . . . . . . . . . . .7

Chapter One: Howard Ervin's Life and Legacy . . . . . .11

Chapter Two: Pentecost's New Voice . . . . . . . . . . . . . .31

Chapter Three: Ervin's Pneumatology . . . . . . . . . . . . .43

Chapter Four: One Baptism–One Filling . . . . . . . . . . .73

Chapter Five: Answering His Critics . . . . . . . . . . . . . .97

Chapter Six: A Call for Re-Examination . . . . . . . . . .127

About the Author . . . . . . . . . . . . . . . . . . . . . . . . . . . .133

Notes . . . . . . . . . . . . . . . . . . . . . . . . . . . . . . . . . . . . . .135

Bibliography . . . . . . . . . . . . . . . . . . . . . . . . . . . . . . . .147

Subject Index . . . . . . . . . . . . . . . . . . . . . . . . . . . . . . .153

Scripture Index . . . . . . . . . . . . . . . . . . . . . . . . . . . . . .157

*Chapter One*

# Howard Ervin's
# Life and Legacy

Howard Matthew Ervin was born into the family of Harry and Florence Ervin on September 21, 1915, in the small coal-mining town of St. Nicholas, Pennsylvania. From his youth, this self-described "practical agnostic" had little interest in religion. Raised in the Dutch Reformed tradition, he grew up reading the Bible but became so stubborn and skeptical that he eventually questioned whether God even existed. After graduating from high school, Howard spent much of his time in his father's barbershop in Mahanoy City, Pennsylvania.[1]

## *Conversion*

One day Dr. Alfred L. Murray of the First Baptist Church in nearby Lansdale was getting his hair cut in Ervin's father's shop[2], and Howard was freely expressing his skepticism. Murray felt drawn to him, and when all the other customers were gone, he questioned Howard: "Why don't you try reading the Bible as if it were true?" Then he asked if Ervin had ever considered going into the ministry. Ervin had his doubts about the Bible, but he knew for sure that he did not want to be a preacher. He told the pastor, "I've never known a preacher who earned his pay."³ What Ervin did not know was that God was on a mission to capture his life for the service of Jesus Christ.

Late one night, Howard returned from his usual socializing with friends after a long day of work at the soap mill. He had been considering Dr. Murray's words and decided to take his challenge. He began reading his Bible, chapter after chapter, for months, but without understanding. Yet he became more aware of his own sin. On one evening, Howard could not sleep. After lying in bed for a while, he decided to try to pray. Though a skeptic, Howard nevertheless often prayed the only prayer he knew. As he began to pray the Lord's Prayer, he reached the words, "Thy will be done," and something stopped him. He repeated the prayer and again was stopped at the words, "Thy will be done." When he tried again to say "Thy will be done," Ervin could sense the presence of evil as he felt a choking sensation in his throat. Finally, something allowed him to submit his life to God, and he was able to finish the prayer.

Later that night, December 23, 1940, Jesus appeared to him in his room. At that moment, Jesus Christ was no longer merely an idea or an historical figure far removed from Howard's life: he had met Jesus face to face. Because of his Pennsylvania Dutch stubbornness, Ervin knew that only this kind of experience with the Lord could bring him to his knees. Howard's agnosticism had not resulted from having investigated Christianity and having found it untrue. Rather, he had simply rejected Jesus because acknowledging Him as Lord would have disturbed his own plans for his life. The next day, Christmas Eve, he told Dr. Murray that he had given his life to Christ and was ready to enter the ministry. Murray was elated at the news, but he was not surprised. That day in the barbershop, God had showed the pastor that Howard Ervin was to be a minister of the gospel.

## *Education*

Young Ervin had always had his mind on higher education. Before his conversion, he had already decided that coal mining and making soap were not for him, and he dreamed of going to law school. But when Ervin accepted God's call to gospel ministry, he knew he would go to seminary. Influenced by Dr. Murray, Ervin enrolled in Eastern Baptist Theological Seminary (EBTS) in Philadelphia, where he earned Bachelor of Arts and Bachelor of Theology degrees.

At EBTS Ervin studied under what he calls a "rare group of men."[4] He credits one professor, Dr. Adams, with transmitting to him the lifelong habit of interpreting Scripture by the maxim, "What does the text say?",[5] even if that leads one, in Ervin's words, to "depart from traditional theology if the text supports it."[6] After Eastern, Ervin earned a Master of Arts in Near Eastern Studies from the Asia Institute and a Bachelor of Divinity from New Brunswick Theological Seminary.[7] As impressive as the previous four degrees were, Ervin went on to receive the Doctor of Theology degree from Princeton Theological Seminary in 1962 while ministering in New Jersey. His dissertation explored the theology of the Psalms in the Septuagint.

## *Early Pastorates*

Although he is a scholar of impeccable credentials, Ervin has a pastor's heart. His first opportunity to pastor came when Dr. Murray was called up to military chaplaincy, and Ervin was asked to replace the pastor who, years earlier, had affirmed God's call to the young skeptic. Ervin served as interim at First Baptist Church in Lansdale for two and one-half years until Dr. Murray returned. Ordination followed on January 17, 1946, by the Northern Baptist Convention (NBC) of New Jersey. A former classmate at EBTS, Richard Shearer, recommended Ervin to succeed him as pastor at Central Baptist Church in Atlantic Highlands, New Jersey; and in February 1946, Ervin left Pennsylvania to accept Central's call. Ervin pastored this congregation for three years, during which he struggled to be effective, despite his eloquence and theological training.[8] While in seminary, Ervin had become aware of the NBC's liberal drift, and, sensing its continuation, he attempted to persuade Central Baptist Church to leave the Convention. When his attempt failed, Ervin felt compelled to leave Central and resigned the pastorate in February 1949.[9] His subsequent founding of Emmanuel Baptist Church attracted Central Baptist members loyal to Ervin, splitting Central Baptist. Years later Ervin would still lament his involvement in the fracturing of that church. In response to it, when he entered the Charismatic Renewal, Ervin's central message became the healing of the Body of Christ.

Ervin served at Emmanuel Baptist Church for the next seventeen years. They were fertile years that would aid his over fifty years of Pentecostal belief and teaching. Ervin pastored Emmanuel Baptist Church throughout his entry into the Charismatic Renewal and until he came to Oral Roberts University in 1966.

## Marriage and Family

While a student at Eastern, Ervin met a fellow student, Marta Vaskis, in the seminary coffee shop. Marta had been born in Latvia and immigrated to London to study during World War II. As he recalls it, when Marta entered the seminary coffee shop for their first meeting, he knew instantly that she was the woman he would marry.[10] Howard and Marta married April 22, 1944. She was the love of his life and a constant companion as God's plan unfolded for their lives. Marta had the tough job of being a pastor's wife through the many changes that happened in his ministry. Marta had earned a B.A. in London during the war, and she also graduated from EBTS with a B.A. Marta ministered alongside her husband when she could. Always graceful and proper, Marta served Howard with love and cared for him and their family until her passing in October of 2004. The dedication in his original volume, *These Are Not Drunken, As Ye Suppose*, expresses his appreciation for her: "Dedication: 'The elder unto the elect and her children whom I love in the truth' (2 John 1 ASV): Marta, Gretchen, Deborah and Judith."[11] Howard and Marta were blessed with three daughters, five grandchildren, and four great-grandchildren.

## Personal Characteristics

Though Howard Ervin the theologian has been a public figure, he has kept his personal life private. Ervin is quick to share the stories of the Holy Spirit's work in his life, but is hesitant to bring attention to himself. He is a tall and handsome man with a gentle voice. His conversations and the way he lives his life show his utmost reverence for God and the Scriptures. In the style of the traditional professor, he has an impressive command of proper English and a scholar's vocabulary. Many say that one needs a thesaurus to speak conversationally to Dr. Ervin. At ORU he is known for his scholarship, decorum, fatherliness, and gentle but authoritative spirit. Even among his colleagues at Oral Roberts University, few call him anything but "Dr. Ervin." Many at the University have looked to Ervin as a role model and mentor.[12] He is always proper, respectful, and professional.

### PILGRIMAGE INTO PENTECOST

Pastor Ervin's commitment to good exegesis made him unable to dismiss the miraculous elements he found in the Scriptures throughout years of study. His dispensationalist Baptist theological training taught him that the time of miracles had passed with the apostles, a view called "cessationism." But because his theology was thoroughly exegetical, he found cessationist views to be insufficient. As Ervin taught verse by verse through the Scriptures, he was unable especially to skip over the inconvenient parts of the Book of Acts. Forced to deal with Acts, Ervin approached the text as objectively as he could.

### *"Theological Discovery of a Lifetime"*

Ervin's Baptist theology had taught him that Pentecost was the birthday of the Church, but he questioned if the Scriptures taught this view. The pivotal moment in his pilgrimage into Pentecost came while studying the Scriptures through the night, until 3:00 a.m. Ervin discovered a crucial correlation he had never noticed before: Jesus breathes on his disciples and gives the Spirit to them, saying "Receive the Holy Spirit" (John 20:22). This gift of the Spirit occurs on the day of his Resurrection but a full fifty days before the Day of Pentecost (Acts 2). Ervin considers this his "theological discovery of a lifetime."[13] He recognized that in John's Gospel Jesus' breath mirrors the creation account of Genesis 12. In Genesis the breath of God makes Adam a living soul (2:7), while in the Gospel of John the breath of the resurrected Jesus regenerates his disciples into the new creation. Ervin recognized that John's Gospel recorded a giving of the Spirit different from the outpouring of the Spirit on the Day of Pentecost. At this discovery, Ervin leaped to his feet and ran to his sleeping wife Marta. As Ervin began sharing his discovery, she replied sleepily, "I have been trying to tell you that for six months."[14]

## *Toward Pentecost*

Ervin was beginning to understand what Luke describes in the Book of Acts. Now he would try to communicate this discovery to his congregation. Though he had not yet experienced a Pentecostal Spirit baptism, he taught his congregation about this experience by teaching verse by verse through Acts. This task was tough and accompanied by many unanswered questions. But Ervin's intellectual honesty kept him from shying away from the tough questions. Soon the congregation began to say to him, "Pastor, you've taught about the baptism; when do we start praying?"[15]

Two significant events led Ervin to genuinely desire baptism in the Holy Spirit. At a conference in 1956, Ervin met a Presbyterian attorney and his wife, Charles and Helen

Maurice. She told about being healed of Hodgkin's disease when a Pentecostal medical doctor prayed for her.[16] This testimony weighed on Ervin because he had recently ministered to a woman in their church who eventually died from this disease. They told about the miraculous power of God they had experienced. The couple also told him of their experience of being baptized in the Holy Spirit and speaking in tongues. This testimony likewise struck a chord in his soul. Clearly, this couple had experienced God in a way that he had not.

The early years of Ervin's pastoral ministry were stressful. As he ministered to his church, he found that his excitement about Christ was beginning to wane, and he also noticed a lack of passion in the members of his church. He dealt daily with the struggles of founding a new church. The Ervin family was also growing with the birth of their daughter, Gretchen, and later the birth of twin girls, Judith and Deborah. The splitting of Central Baptist Church also weighed heavily on this young pastor. Finishing a seminary degree and pursuing a doctorate taxed his time and energy. All these forces left him feeling empty.

His theology was consistently being challenged as he tried to stay faithful to the Scriptures. This commitment to the text brought him to realize that he was living well beneath the experience of the earliest believers portrayed in the New Testament. He recalls, "When I read the Scriptures it made my own experience seem like another world. If my experience was normative, there was something wrong with the Scriptures. If the Scriptures were normative, there was something wrong with my experience and the experience of the church as I know it."[17] At times he had become so desperate for something to change in his life that he would even pray for God to fill him with the Spirit. However, he resisted praying for the baptism in the Spirit because he knew he risked the heresy of speaking with tongues.

Three years after his first encounter with Charles and Helen, they began sending to Ervin issues of *The Voice,* the magazine of the Full Gospel Business Men's Fellowship International (FGBMFI). Opening the first issue, it fell open to a picture of his Presbyterian friend.[18] He began to read the testimonies of others who had received the Holy Spirit. Additionally, Charles sent Ervin the testimonies of Dr. Tommy Tyson, a Methodist pastor, and Dr. John Osteen, a Baptist pastor. He also heard the testimony of Harald Bredesen, a Lutheran minister who lived near him in New York. Like Ervin, Bredesen had discovered the baptism in the Spirit through his own study. And the testimonies of all these included another element of Ervin's experience: All of them struggled with emptiness in their ministry and were looking for the fullness of the Holy Spirit before they experienced Spirit baptism.

After learning about the baptism in the Spirit from these men, he decided to look at the Book of Acts once again. This time, as he read the story of the Day of Pentecost, it all began to make sense. Ervin began to ask God, "How soon can I have the experience? Don't leave anything out or I am going to feel cheated. I don't want to wait till it becomes popular. Let it cost me something."[19] Shortly after, Ervin heard that a well known Pentecostal named David du Plessis was to speak at Ervin's alma mater, Princeton Theological Seminary. Ervin knew he had to see him. Ervin met du Plessis that weekend and instantly felt a rapport with him. David graciously answered all of Ervin's questions and asked Ervin if he could pray with him. This was the first time he had experienced Pentecostal prayer, and the two would eventually become lifelong friends.

Following this meeting, Ervin knew he had to meet with Harald Bredesen in nearby Mt. Vernon, New York. He wrote to ask if he could visit. Bredesen invited Ervin, and when they met and visited a while, Bredesen prayed for Ervin, but nothing discernible happened. Ervin left the meeting feeling anxious. He returned to the church reluctantly for an evening deacon meeting. When the deacons began to pray, Ervin began to experience "liquid love" coming all over him unexpectedly.[20] Ervin sensed God's presence in a new way, causing him to say later that for the first time he had "learned how to worship."[21] Ervin had tasted the Spirit's power.

## *Baptized in the Spirit*

Ervin completed his pilgrimage into Pentecost in 1960. After a year and nine months of careful investigation and prayer, Ervin was baptized in the Holy Spirit. He had been invited by one of his deacons to a FGBMFI meeting in Miami, Florida.[22] After one of the sessions, Ervin met with David du Plessis and Dennis Bennett in his hotel room in order to pray to receive the baptism in the Spirit. Though other men had prayed with Ervin before, du Plessis and Bennett wanted to lay hands on him. When these men began to pray for him, Ervin felt ten thousand volts of divine electricity go through him. Later that night, Ervin awakened in bed, soaked in sweat. He could still feel the fire of the Spirit all over his body. Ervin decided to cool down with a shower. He says, "As I stepped out of the shower and pulled a towel around my shoulders, I heard words rolling inside me. . . . Then I had a vision of a ticker tape."[23] What he saw in his head was a language he did not know. As he began to speak the words that he saw, a beautiful language rolled off his tongue. What he had read about in the Scriptures and heard about through the testimonies of others had finally happened to him. Although his pilgrimage into Pentecost was complete, his journey into Pentecostalism had just begun.

## *Ministering the Spirit*

How would he bring this experience of Spirit baptism back to his Baptist church in New Jersey? Remembering the lessons of his experience at Central Baptist, Ervin was very careful not to allow his experience to fracture Emmanuel Baptist Church. Although he had been teaching the church about Spirit baptism, he was not ready to integrate this new experience into his regular ministry. People who were interested in this experience would come to his home office rather than to the church. When a church member was ready to be baptized in the Spirit, he would invite them to his office, a converted coal bin in the parsonage basement. He would seat them in what he called the "hot seat,"[24] so named because so many were baptized in the Holy Spirit sitting on it. As more and more people became interested, Ervin decided to add a prayer meeting after the Sunday evening service. Ervin always led a traditionally Baptist Sunday morning service but also began offering a Pentecostal healing prayer service after the Sunday night service.[25] These prayer meetings went on for three years and would regularly last until midnight, sometimes until 3:00 a.m. Through the ministries of the "hot seat" and the healing service, many in his congregation experienced Spirit baptism, physical healing, and other answers to prayer.

The word about these meetings began to spread to surrounding communities, and Emmanuel Baptist Church eventually offered an ecumenical ministry to people of every denomination who were open to the Spirit. Ervin was even featured in an article in the *Saturday Evening Post* about denominational pastors who spoke in tongues.[26] The late-night healing services were attended by visitors ranging from "Quakers to Catholics, a number of whom traveled fifty miles and more to attend the charismatic services."[27] In these times of ecumenical ministry, Ervin became convinced that the outpouring of the Holy Spirit was God's answer to the problem of denominational strife. He says, "The number one priority of the Holy Spirit is the healing of the Church."[28] Through partnership with FGBMFI and men such as Demos Shakarian, David du Plessis, Harald Bredesen, and Oral Roberts, Howard Ervin was able to bring the message of baptism in the Holy Spirit to people from every theological tradition. His new interest in the ecumenical nature of the Charismatic Renewal made Ervin the perfect man for Oral Roberts to include in his multi-denominational Partners Seminars.

## *Toward Tulsa*

In 1963, Oral Roberts held his first Partners' Seminar on the new campus of Oral Roberts University (ORU) in Tulsa,

Oklahoma. People from eleven different denominations attended, unified by their desire to evangelize and to help others be baptized in the Holy Spirit.[29] The second Partners' Seminar was held a few months later in April 1964, and Howard Ervin was one of the speakers.[30] Oral was impressed by Ervin's credentials as a scholar and his testimony as a Spirit-filled believer. While Ervin was still serving Emmanuel Baptist Church, Oral invited him to be an advisor in the creation of ORU'S School of Theology.[31] Ervin established a great friendship with Oral Roberts as he spoke at other Partner's Seminars and FGBMFI meetings around the country. This seminar began a relationship between Dr. Ervin and Oral Roberts University that would last over forty years.

**TEACHING AT ORAL ROBERTS UNIVERSITY**

Although Ervin pastored for twenty years, he had dreamed of being a professor. This dream was realized in 1966 when he joined the faculty of the nation's first Charismatic university, Oral Roberts University. Ervin was asked personally by Oral Roberts and Dr. R. O. Corvin to be one of the founding members of the theology faculty at ORU.[32] The founder and first president of Oral Roberts University commented that when building the university, "God knew I needed Howard Ervin."[33] Because of his impeccable credentials, he was quickly drawn into leadership and served as the associate dean of the School of Theology.[34] In the summer of 1967, Howard Ervin was appointed the dean of the School of Theology.

As he quickly encountered the challenges of running a new seminary, Ervin believed that the young university was not ready for a seminary. Problems with accreditation in 1968 led Ervin to ask Oral to close the seminary. With the seminary closed, Ervin began the process of building an undergraduate theology department. Howard Ervin served as the chairman of the Department of Theology from 1969 to 1978 and designed an excellent academic undergraduate program. Eventually the new seminary, the School of Theology and Missions, opened, and Ervin joined the faculty as Professor of Old Testament. Ervin served on the Faculty Council and was the seminary's most senior and respected member of the faculty. Though well qualified for administrative leadership, he preferred his first love of teaching.

Dr. Ervin taught in his two areas of expertise, Old Testament and pneumatology. One class became known as his signature class, GTHE 692: Pneumatology. It was the crown of his forty-year academic career. The content of this study on Pentecostal pneumatology, combined with his wealth of experience in the Charismatic Renewal, made this class educational and enlightening for graduate theology students. The class not only explored Ervin's view of pneumatology theologically and exegetically, but it also transmitted his stories of how God had moved so powerfully in his own life. Dr. Ervin never lost his pastor's heart when he entered the classroom. His credentials brought him credibility, but his life brought authenticity to his message.

During his forty-year teaching career at ORU, Howard Ervin received multiple university awards for outstanding teaching, so many that he finally asked the current dean of the School of Theology and Missions, Dr. Thomson Mathew, to remove his name from the ballot used to determine the school's annual teaching award.³⁵ In 2006, the school and the university capped Ervin's career at ORU by awarding him the seminary's and the university's outstanding teaching awards.³⁶ Ervin retired from his duties as professor in the fall semester of 2006 at 91 years of age. He is still beloved by faculty and students. This writer was privileged to be part of Dr. Ervin's final Pneumatology class, in the spring of 2006. At the time of this writing, Dr. Ervin is 92 years of age and still as articulate and challenging as any professor in the School of Theology and Missions.

## ECUMENICAL IMPACT

Despite his affirming a Pentecostal view of Spirit baptism, Howard Ervin interacted with Pentecostal denominations much less than he did with members of many other denominations in the Charismatic Renewal of the 1960's and 1970's. Through the FGBMFI and Oral Roberts Ministries' (ORM) Partner Seminars, Ervin led thousands of believers from all denominations into the Spirit-filled life. At the seminars, Oral always insisted that Ervin lead ministry offered in the Holy Spirit Room. Ministering to believers from many church traditions, Ervin learned a great lesson: that "the number one priority of the Holy Spirit is the healing of the Church."³⁷

Ervin was filled with the Spirit as a result of the Charismatic Renewal of the 1960s through the 1980s. Contemporaries have labeled Ervin a Charismatic and a Neo-Pentecostal. Ervin, however, has never been comfortable with these titles. The gospel of Spirit baptism that he preached to believers of all traditions correlated to classical

Pentecostal teaching much more than it did to other views of Spirit baptism spawned through the Charismatic and Third-Wave Renewals. It featured a belief in subsequence to conversion as Spirit baptism's timing, tongues-speech as its immediately observable evidence, and empowerment for witness as its purpose. Ervin has many questions about the direction of today's Charismatic Movement and has distanced himself from the label "Charismatic."

He saw very early that the Charismatic Renewal was becoming a movement, creating its own new churches more than encouraging participants to remain within their pre-Charismatic traditions, which was his prayer for them and his own practice. Although Ervin never joined a Pentecostal denomination, his theology always remained classical Pentecostal. He is unashamedly Pentecostal and Baptist, believing that the gift of the Holy Spirit is for the whole church, not just Pentecostal denominations, and that the Holy Spirit does not divide but unites the church.

## Dialogue with Rome

Although fully involved in the Charismatic Renewal, Ervin was never caught up into the emotionalism typical of the Pentecostal and Charismatic Movements. He always maintained a high-church demeanor in his ministry. Ervin was considered a friend of Sacramentalists, and his formal style was appreciated by the Catholic Charismatics. Charismatic Presbyterian theologian Charles Farrah noted that "Catholics particularly responded to his quiet and effective ministry."[38] Ervin became convinced that Pentecostal pneumatology had more in common with Roman Catholic than evangelical theology. He expresses this conviction in his response to James Dunn's critique of Pentecostal theology, in which Ervin defends not only Pentecostalism, but also various sacramental views.[39]

Ervin's reverence for God and ecumenical attitude sent him as an ambassador for the Spirit-filled life to sheep in different theological pastures. Remarkably, Ervin the Spirit-filled Baptist has ministered at events for the Roman Catholic Charismatic Movement far more often than at Pentecostal events. After the passing of Pope John Paul I, August 1978, Ervin was present at the St. Nicholas Catholic Charismatic Center in Houston, Texas, and found himself in the surprising position of being a Baptist minister offering condolences and comfort to a grieving body of Roman Catholics.

In Tulsa, Ervin filled the role of shepherd to many Charismatic Roman Catholics. When the Catholic Charismatic Movement began in Tulsa, Father Francis MacNutt was invited to Oral Roberts University. Fr. MacNutt was asked by the Roman Catholics who had received the Pentecostal experience to help them form a fellowship in Tulsa. Fr. MacNutt insisted that Ervin be the advisor and group leader for the first Catholic Charismatic group in Tulsa.[40] Many of these Catholic believers in Tulsa considered Ervin their "father."[41] For many years, Ervin would host a weekly Bible study in his home for those who were experiencing the Charismatic Renewal in traditional, mainline churches. Whether in his healing services at Emmanuel or during ministry to Catholic Charismatics, Ervin emphatically insisted that these believers stay in their own denominations. He would even discourage Catholics who wished to be baptized in water and insisted that they remain faithful to their own communions. Jesus prayed in John 17 for the unity of His disciples, and Ervin believed that this prayer for the healing unity of the Church would be realized through Spirit-filled believers in every tradition.

Through his friendship with David du Plessis, Ervin was invited to participate in the Pentecostal–Roman Catholic Dialogues. Du Plessis asked Ervin to participate because he knew that Ervin could articulate the Pentecostal position theologically. During the years of 1979 to 1987, Ervin participated and represented the Pentecostal point of view. In 1979 and 1987, he represented the Pentecostal viewpoint on the subjects of hermeneutics and *koinonia*. His service was historic, because the steering committee voted in 1976 to have only Pentecostals serve as Pentecostal participants.[42] Despite his Baptist identity, Ervin's Pentecostal theology, his scholarly and formal communication style, and his ecumenical beliefs made him the exception to the rule.

Ervin exemplifies being ecumenical, but this has not always been his history. When he began his ministry, as a good Baptist he was quite prejudiced against many of the liturgical traditions. Like Saul of Tarsus, Ervin admits that he had been the worst of those who were anti-Catholic.[43] Ervin grew up in a time and in a part of Pennsylvania where there was deep distrust, even animosity, between Protestants and Catholics.[44] Ironically, early in the revival at Emmanuel, Ervin found himself praying for an Episcopalian man with a Catholic wife to receive the baptism in the Spirit.[45] This confused him because in his evangelicalism, he really did not believe that they were even saved. He comments, "My problem was this. I was an evangelical Baptist, I had received the baptism in the Holy Spirit, and I was having all kinds of problems sorting out my theology."[46]

Through his pilgrimage into Pentecost, the Holy Spirit melted his heart for believers of all traditions. He truly believes that the Pentecostal movement is the vehicle to bring all denominations together in unity, that theological dogma divides, but that the Spirit unites the Church: "The Pentecostal walk in the Spirit forces one inexorably to reexamine all sectarian dogma in the light of the overarching unity of the Spirit which they experience with other Christians of the most diverse theological backgrounds."[47] Through the Spirit, theology and experience can unite so that Christian doctrine becomes more than just dogma. What the apostles experienced became what they taught. When Christians from different traditions experience the same work of the Spirit, they are united by this common experience, despite their diverse and sometimes conflicting theologies. Theology, as important as it truly is, remains a second-order enterprise that builds upon first-order experience of the Living God, which Ervin believes, with Pentecostals and Charismatics, that Spirit baptism is. Ervin the anti-Catholic evangelical Baptist became ecumenical because of his Pentecostal experience. His Pentecostal conversion resulted in thousands of believers' from traditions outside Pentecostal churches experiencing the Holy Spirit through his ministry.

Ervin never left his Baptist heritage, remaining to this day an American Baptist. As soon as he moved his family to Tulsa to work at ORU, Ervin joined an American Baptist church and involved himself in the Charismatic wing of the

American Baptist Church. Ervin was a keynote speaker at the first American Baptist Conference on the Holy Spirit, in 1975, where he gave a "Rationale for Tongues."[48] Dr. Gary Clark, the long-time chairman of the Holy Spirit Renewal Ministries in American Baptist Churches, worked with Ervin in those early days. He says, "He was the patriarch of the movement, definitely. He was the trained, Th.D.-from-Princeton theologian. He was the biblical authority. We wanted him to give us the biblical foundation. . . . He was very influential and his teaching was very good. It was the solid basis on which the early years of the American Baptist Movement were built."[49]

From his own denomination to the Roman Catholic Church, Ervin's ministry reached all of the body of Christ. As different groups were introduced to Howard Ervin, they looked to him for leadership because of his knowledge and experience. Perhaps because he never joined a Pentecostal denomination, Ervin was able to reach an even wider population of people with the Pentecostal message.

## Chapter Two

## Pentecost's
# New Voice

Pentecostal and Charismatic biblical scholarship has increased in the last half of the twentieth century. At the beginning of this movement, Howard M. Ervin became one of the first to argue for a unique Lukan pneumatology. Based on his insight that each author in the Bible has to be understood on his own terms, Ervin argued against the evangelical tendency that attempts to synthesize the whole canon of Scripture prematurely, before appreciating the distinctive views of New Testament writers. Scholars after Ervin who have contributed to Pentecostal pneumatology through Luke-Acts studies have stood on Ervin's shoulders, especially in their agreement with his key assumptions and methods. Luke's Gospel and the Book of Acts express an understanding of the Spirit distinct from that of other writers. Ervin's exegetical assumption, while not original with him and now commonplace in biblical studies and biblical theology, nevertheless proved groundbreaking for studies in the area of Luke-Acts. Pentecostal-charismatic scholarship and these movements have benefited greatly from these insights.

Dr. Thomson Mathew, dean of the School of Theology and Missions at Oral Roberts University, points out that "[i]t is almost fashionable to be a Pentecostal today. This is not our history. . . . [But] at such a time, God raised up Dr. Howard Ervin to produce the first academic, exegetical defense of the Pentecostal experience that our critics had to respect."[50] Mathew considers Ervin to be "the most articulate defender of Pentecostalism."[51] Mathew admits that at times Dr. Ervin would be considered even more Pentecostal than he, a third-generation Indian Pentecostal preacher.

Henry I. Lederle, in his book *Treasures Old and New*, identifies Ervin as a leader in the Neo-Pentecostal tradition. He remarks, "In *These Are Not Drunken, As Ye Suppose* Howard Ervin presents a defense of the neo-Pentecostal position, one of the earliest scholarly accounts available."[52] The noted Assemblies of God scholar William Menzies remarks, "in the 1960's, there were few engaged in serious academic efforts to present the classical Pentecostal view of Spirit baptism. Ervin was one of the early 'pioneers' of this enterprise. His work was a great encouragement to me as a young, budding Pentecostal professor. He ably engaged dissident views, such as those held by Gordon Fee and James Dunn. This was an important influence on my own studies. I owe him a great debt of gratitude."[53]

Ervin will be best known in the academic world for his 1968 treatise on Pentecostalism, *These Are Not Drunken, As Ye Suppose*.[54] His contributions to the discussion of Pentecostal theology and in particular the theology of Luke-Acts helped contribute to a major shift in New Testament studies. Pentecostal biblical scholar Paul Elbert, who compiled a *Festschrift* in honor of Dr. Ervin's sixty-fifth birthday, says that "Howard did a good job at that particular moment in history in expressing views that were new and I thought were good and right. . . . I thought this man's work was worthy of compliments."[55] Elbert believed that Ervin was a pioneer in interpreting Luke-Acts. Elbert recognized that the non-Pentecostal evangelical worldview dominated New Testament studies and that Ervin was able to open the door to evangelical discussion of Pentecostal pneumatology on the basis of his good exegesis: "Dr. Ervin will be warmly remembered as being in the forefront of those scholars who have entered into this historically neglected area. Stepping into the gap with fresh considerations he exposed the weak underpinnings of theories which unduly confined the Holy Spirit to a restricted range of activity."[56] Elbert recognized that Ervin's perspective on the unique theology offered by Luke was groundbreaking for Pentecostal scholarship: "I regarded him as a pioneer in terms of interpreting Luke-Acts at a time when, in the United States, there was a lot of polemic coming from the larger publishing houses against looking at Luke-Acts this way."[57]

Elbert compiled this commemorative volume with articles from scholars who were also involved in similar work in the area of Luke-Acts. Many of these scholars, such as James Forbes, F. F. Bruce, and James Dunn, recognized Ervin's contribution to Pentecostal scholarship. Forbes remembers: "At a time when I was looking for a solid biblical/theological foundation in support of my faith and experience, I was greatly helped by the scholarly efforts of Howard Ervin."[58] Even James Dunn comments, "His work on the Holy Spirit has provided both a challenge to scholarship and an opportunity for dialogue for those seeking to understand this dimension of our Christian faith."⁵⁹ Even when his critics disagreed with him, they respected Ervin's contributions.

Historically, Pentecostals have offered defenses for their faith, but until Ervin published his work, very little Pentecostal scholarship gave an exegetical and theological foundation for Spirit baptism. Ervin not only defended Pentecostal experience exegetically, but he also critiqued evangelical scholarship that tended to dismiss Pentecostal perspectives. Robert W. Graves, president of the Foundation for Pentecostal Scholarship, remarks, "Between Carl Brumback's *What Meaneth This?* (1947) and Ervin's *These Are Not Drunken, As Ye Suppose* (1967), I am aware of no substantial Pentecostal defenses, and when Ervin's was published, it took the Pentecostal polemic to another level, rendering Brumback's defense, which was already dated, obsolete."⁶⁰ At this time, Pentecostals were just beginning to defend this once-maligned faith in the academic marketplace of ideas. Graves comments, "To my knowledge, no Pentecostal, neo-Pentecostal, or Charismatic has matched Ervin's production of quality Pentecostal literature defending the distinctive doctrines of the continuity of the gifts of the Spirit and the baptism in the Holy Spirit as a subsequent Christian experience signaled by glossolalic utterances while bringing power for witness and service."⁶¹ It is high praise that this Baptist pastor with a Th.D. from Princeton would have so much influence on classical Pentecostal scholarship.

Pentecostal biblical scholars such as Roger Stronstad, Robert Menzies, and James Shelton have advanced the discussion of Lukan pneumatology, with no small debt to Howard Ervin. By acknowledging the distinctiveness of Luke's theology, Pentecostals were able to argue the biblical case for contemporary Pentecostal experience much more effectively than in the past. In their scholarly hands, Lukan pneumatology yields significant support for the Pentecostal view of the Spirit baptism's subsequence, evidence, and empowerment. These features of Spirit baptism lie at the core of Ervin's arguments against the non-Pentecostal evangelical views of conversion-initiation, which have usually been formed out of Pauline theology, without giving Lukan theology its due.

### DIALOGUE WITH JAMES D. G. DUNN

In 1970 James Dunn, noted New Testament scholar and professor of divinity at the University of Durham, published a major book on the Holy Spirit. His *Baptism in the Holy Spirit* is considered one of the best treatments of the evangelical view of Spirit baptism written with the Pentecostal view taken much more seriously than previous evangelical treatments.[62] In it, Dunn argues for the view that Spirit baptism belongs within Christian conversion-initiation and is not an empowerment for service subsequent to conversion-initiation, as asserted in classical Pentecostal theology. Published just two years after Ervin's *These Are Not Drunken, As Ye Suppose*, Dunn's *Baptism in the Spirit* interacts with Ervin's work as one of the Pentecostal sources for his critique. It is not known how Dunn, a professor in England, became exposed to Ervin's work, but he critiqued Ervin's views energetically. Dunn refers to Ervin in relation to the

Pentecostal view of Spirit baptism twelve times.[63] On one occasion, Dunn singles out Ervin in particular with cutting criticism: "His [Ervin's] treatment of [Acts] 4:31 involves some rather unnatural and tortuous exegesis which cannot be accepted."[64] Dunn also commends Ervin for deviating from most Pentecostals on Paul's understanding of being baptized into one body,[65] and he critiques Ervin's view of once-for-all Spirit baptism in his conclusion.[66] Although Dunn deals with several Pentecostal sources in addition to Ervin, including Gordon Lindsay (1964), Larry Christenson (1964), and Ralph M. Riggs (1949), Dunn focuses on Ervin's distinctive view of "One Baptism-One Filling" and his treatment of Acts 4:31.[67]

In November of 1980, the Society for Pentecostal Studies met on the campus of Oral Roberts University in Tulsa, Oklahoma. Robert Graves took time during the meeting to interview Howard Ervin about James Dunn's treatment of his work. Some ten years after Dunn's critique of Pentecostalism, Ervin had not yet read the book or even given much consideration to Dunn's arguments. Ervin told Graves, "I am aware that he has made some references, but I've never even checked them out."[68] Graves pointed out Dunn's objections to the Pentecostal view of Spirit baptism and asked Ervin to respond. After discussing each of Dunn's arguments, it became clear that someone needed to answer Dunn. Graves encouraged him to write a rebuttal. Being one who enjoys a good theological debate, Ervin concluded, "I'll have to do a critique."[69]

This meeting prompted Ervin to write what would become his most widely quoted work. Robert Graves recalls, "A few months after I interviewed Dr. Ervin, I received a package in the mail; to my complete surprise, it was the first chapter of *Conversion-Initiation*. As you can tell from the interview, he showed no intentions of replying to Dunn, had not even read Dunn. When I asked him about it, he said my visit 'crystallized' in his mind the need for a response."[70] Consequently, in the Foreword of *Conversion-Initiation and Baptism in the Holy Spirit*, Dr. Ervin gives "a special word of appreciation" to Robert Graves because his "comments and shared research have made a significant contribution to the formulation of the views expressed at the critical points in the discussion."[71] This new work was formulated during one Christmas break, more than a decade after his first defense of Pentecostalism.[72] Once again Dr. Ervin took on the task of defending Pentecostalism before its scholarly critics. Ervin's two critical works gave legitimacy to the Pentecostal message. *Conversion-Initiation and Baptism in the Holy Spirit* would eventually become a rallying point for Pentecostals responding to Dunn and other evangelicals; and many other critiques of anti-Pentecostal views authored by other Pentecostal and Charismatic scholars would follow.

In *Conversion-Initiation and Baptism in the Holy Spirit*, Ervin critiques and rebuts Dunn in "an examination of the inadequacies and errors in the exegesis offered in support of the conversion-initiation thesis. I have simply accepted the gauntlet wherever Dr. Dunn has thrown it down."[73] Ervin exposes the presuppositions governing anti-Pentecostal evangelical theology and shows that these do not arise from sound exegesis. He argues for a unique Lukan pneumatology that relates Spirit baptism to conversion-initiation rather than to empowerment for the continuation of the kingdom ministry of Jesus. Overall, the book responds with a consistent Pentecostal view to Dunn's arguments, but Ervin also takes the opportunity to rebut Dunn wherever he critiques Ervin's particular views: "Inasmuch as Professor Dunn had singled out my views on Acts 4:8, 31, and 13:9 for rebuttal, a personal response is in order."[74] In this chapter, Ervin defends his exegesis of the passages in Acts that many read as describing fillings of the Spirit subsequent to Spirit baptism.

Ervin's works succeeded in confronting the largely non-Pentecostal world of Christian biblical and theological scholarship with serious proposals in favor of Pentecostal belief and practice. Before Ervin, Pentecostalism was dismissed by most Christian religious academicians as an experiential faith based on bad exegesis resulting from its proponents' lacking education. Ervin not only demonstrated that Pentecostals fit within a stream of evangelicalism but also that Pentecostal pneumatology is grounded in good biblical exegesis. Following Ervin's pioneering scholarship, Pentecostal scholars are now able to engage evangelical and other Christian theological scholarship effectively in critique and appreciation and contributing to new ecumenical scholarship of Luke-Acts. Now not only Pentecostals but also evangelicals and scholars from other Christian traditions find their pneumatologies under the microscope, and all benefit from distinguishing more clearly between presuppositions scholars bring to their work and the biblical exegesis that should underpin their theology.

## OVERVIEW OF WORKS

Howard Ervin is not only an educator and pastor, but he is also a capable writer. He produced six scholarly books on the subject of pneumatology between 1968 and 2002. In 1968, Ervin produced *These Are Not Drunken, As Ye Suppose,* his first work on the Pentecostal experience of the Spirit.[75] It outlines all that Dr. Ervin learned and taught in his church on the subject of Spirit baptism. Considered one of the first scholarly works from a Pentecostal position, this work makes a strong exegetical argument for the missionary purpose of the baptism in the Holy Spirit, for tongues as its initial observable evidence, for his distinctive understanding that one experiences only one Spirit baptism identical with one Spirit filling, and for his exposition of spiritual gifts. The tone and spirit of this text is apologetic. Ervin systematically explains each of the issues of Spirit baptism and its expression in the Book of Acts. This work is written for the pastor or educator and masterfully reflects the practical and theological arguments of Ervin's pneumatology.

In 1971, Ervin published a series of letters that he had written to a member of his former congregation. *And Forbid Not to Speak with Tongues* contains answers to Tony's questions prompted by Dr. J. Vernon McGee's critique of tongues.[76] Ervin answers pastorally the questions raised by McGee's anti-Pentecostal views. This short book was written to be understandable by the layman and is easy to read. Ervin shows his ability to expose the exegesis and presuppositions of anti-Pentecostals.

In 1972, Logos Publishing released his third work, *That Which Ye See and Hear*.[77] As a series of essays, Ervin discusses further issues brought about by questions raised in his first work. This work goes beyond exegesis to practical and philosophical issues raised after his first work. It offers a broader rationale for tongues and discusses the role of dogma in the Pentecostal faith. He discusses topics such as an understanding of the full metaphor of Spirit baptism, the purpose of Pentecost, and tongues as prophecy and signs.

The same year, Ervin contributed to *The Layman's Commentary on the Holy Spirit,* edited by his friend and colleague, John Rea.[78] Ervin was one of the contributing editors, along with R. O. Corvin, the original dean of the School of Theology at ORU, David du Plessis, and J. Rodman Williams. This work comments on important biblical passages pertinent to the Holy Spirit, but as a multi-contributor work edited to express a single voice and style, Ervin's contributions cannot be distinguished from those of the other editors.

In 1984, Ervin responded to Dunn's *Baptism in the Holy Spirit* with his work, *Conversion-Initiation and Baptism in the Holy Spirit.*[79] This work provides an argument-by-argument critique of Dunn's treatment of Pentecostal theology. With additional exegetical support for the Pentecostal viewpoint and a defense of his own views, Ervin shows how the Pentecostal exegesis is sound and consistent. Simple arguments as well as complex exegesis make this work important for any Pentecostal looking for solid defense of their faith.

In 1987 Ervin republished his classic work *These Are Not Drunken, As Ye Suppose* as *Spirit Baptism: A Biblical Investigation.*[80] This work re-organizes and clarifies some of his best arguments. With added clarity and additional exegetical arguments, as well as a restructuring of the progression of the book, *Spirit Baptism* provides a fresh look at Ervin's Pentecostal theology and is an excellent addition to the Pentecostal library. Ervin updated his arguments using newer and better sources not available to him when the original work was produced. This book provides the same scholarship but adds the insights made over the ensuing twenty years of speaking, lecturing, and teaching. With a logical progression and clear arguments, it remains one of the best explanations of Pentecostalism.

In 2002, Ervin published his latest book, *Healing: Sign of the Kingdom*.[81] This book outlines clearly his understanding of healing as the sign of the kingdom of God. He argues that Jesus preached only one message: the gospel of the kingdom of God. This message was followed by signs that confirmed this message. He tackles the difficult issues of the relationship between faith and healing. His views on the difference between signs and wonders and spiritual gifts of healing are some of the most insightful contributions to the discussion of spiritual gifts. The book is well written with easy-to-follow arguments. At just over a hundred pages, it is a great work for the scholar or layman.

Ervin also published a number of articles over the years. Many of them are listed in *Essays on Apostolic Themes*, edited by Paul Elbert. Ervin wrote several articles for the Full Gospel Business Men's Fellowship International, for Assemblies of God publications, and for Oral Roberts Ministries. Ervin also published an article in *Pnuema: The Journal for the Society for Pentecostal Studies* called

"Hermeneutics: a Pentecostal Option" that was reprinted in *Essays on Apostolic Themes*. Ervin also presented at several meetings of the Society for Pentecostal Studies. Some of these presentations were integrated into the book *Conversion-Initiation and Baptism in the Holy Spirit*.

# Chapter Three

## Ervin's
# Pneumatology

Howard M. Ervin will be remembered for providing one of the first defenses of the Pentecostal faith. His contributions are unique in that Ervin offers a theological and exegetical apologetic for each of the Pentecostal distinctives. Ervin argues convincingly that Luke has a unique pneumatology. He believes that, for Luke, to be filled with the Spirit is an empowering experience with the Spirit that is subsequent to salvation and is evidenced by speaking in tongues. Each argument is backed by sound exegesis.

While many Pentecostal scholars have gone to scholarship to validate their own Pentecostal experience, Howard Ervin's testimony is quite the opposite. Ervin's "Pilgrimage into Pentecost" began in the Scriptures. Because of his theological training, he always endeavored to find out what the text says without imposing theological presuppositions on the text. Ervin has always been able to depart from traditional theological dogma when he believed the text supported it. As he studied the Scriptures he was confronted by the truth of the text.

## BAPTISM IN THE HOLY SPIRIT

The term used by Pentecostals for the event subsequent to salvation is commonly called "Baptism in the Holy Spirit." This is a reflection of Jesus' promise, "For John baptized with water, but in a few days you will be baptized with the Holy Spirit" (Acts 1:5). Some Pentecostals make a distinction between being "baptized" in the Holy Spirit and being "filled" with the Spirit. For evangelicals, being baptized in the Spirit is commonly understood as salvation, while being filled with the Spirit is related more to empowerment or holy living. Ervin points out that this sort of approach to defining these terms is based more in a theological presupposition than it is on good exegesis. In order to understand what the experience of baptism in the Holy Spirit is, one must first determine how the term is used in context. Ervin is convinced that for Luke, baptism in the Spirit is synonymous with being filled with the Spirit. This filling of the Spirit is subsequent to the conversion work of the Spirit and is for the purpose of empowering believers for the work of the kingdom. To begin with, Ervin keenly points out that the use of the term "baptism" in relation to the Holy Spirit occurs only three times in Luke-Acts: once by John (Luke 3:16); once by Jesus (Acts 1:5); and once by Peter, who remembers Jesus' words (Acts 11:16).[82] Each time it is used, it is a phrase used by Jesus. However, Luke never uses the term "baptism" in relation to the Holy Spirit when he records in his own words the events that fulfill Jesus' promise. This metaphor of baptism is exclusive to Jesus' description of the Pentecost event. In Acts 1:8, Jesus says that they will be "baptized in the Holy Spirit," but Acts 2:4 records that they were "all filled with the Holy Spirit." Luke chooses to use other terms to communicate the phenomenon of what Jesus described as a baptism in the Holy Spirit.

Ervin believes that this connection is crucial to understanding the relationship between "baptism" in the Holy Spirit and being "filled" with the Spirit. He notes, "In every other place where Luke made reference to the Pentecostal baptism in the Holy Spirit, he employed such phrases as the 'Holy Spirit came upon,' 'filled with the Holy Spirit,' 'received the Holy Spirit,' 'the Holy Spirit fell upon,' and 'the gift of the Holy Spirit was poured out.'"[83] Ervin believes that terms used for each of these events signify that each recapitulates the Pentecost event.

Therefore, there is a univocal relationship between being baptized in the Holy Spirit and being filled with the Spirit. These two terms describe the same reality: that is, Pentecost. Ervin says, "Contextually, the terms baptized in the Holy Spirit and filled with the Holy Spirit are used interchangeably as related aspects of the same experience."[84] So then, if one is baptized in the Spirit, for Luke one is filled with the Spirit, and vice versa. Again, to Ervin, it is an issue of proper exegesis. If Jesus said "baptism" and Luke called it "filled," then the terms are synonymous. Both terms are phrases used to depict the empowering dimension of the Spirit that they had not yet encountered.

Any understanding of subsequent stories of persons' being baptized in the Spirit must be grounded in the initial Pentecostal event. Each subsequent story is a recapitulation of the Pentecost event in a different context. This is illustrated in Acts 10, when Cornelius and his household receive the Spirit, and in Acts 11, when Peter is describing that event. Luke records that the Holy Spirit "came on" the disciples (Acts 10:44). Later Peter defends this action as being the same event that happened to them on the Day of Pentecost. He says, "As I began to speak, the Holy Spirit came on them as he had come on us at the beginning. Then I remembered what the Lord had said: 'John baptized with water, but you will be baptized with the Holy Spirit.' So if God gave them the same gift as he gave us, who believed in the Lord Jesus Christ, who was I to think that I could oppose God?" (Acts 11:15–17). Here is a case where the same event Jesus describes as a "baptism" is described with another metaphor, "come upon." Luke's terms are different than Jesus' terms. It is a filling in Acts 2:4 and a coming upon in Acts 11:15. But both are attributed to the one Pentecostal experience Jesus calls a "baptism with the Holy Spirit." Ervin says, "By his choice of words, Peter therefore stressed the identical nature of the two experiences."[85] The context of each of these events in Acts would prove the terms are in fact synonymous. Ervin continues: "Luke, in recording the phenomenology of the event, wrote, 'they were all filled with the Holy Spirit.' It is no homiletical extravagance to conclude, therefore, that baptism in the Spirit = filled with the Spirit. The message is clear enough."[86] If Luke chose to use the term "filled" in response to what happened on the day of Pentecost, then Luke equates "baptism" in the Holy Spirit with being "filled" with the Spirit. He says, "Things equal to the same thing are equal to each other."[87] This is the heart of Ervin's understanding of Acts. Each event where someone is "filled with the Spirit" is a Pentecost event. If one does not make the connection between the two terms, it can lead to a theology where Luke's terms mean different aspects of the Spirit's work. It may also lead one to misunderstand the nature of Spirit baptism itself.

### THE BIRTHDAY OF THE CHURCH

Central to the debate between evangelicals and Pentecostals over Spirit baptism is the question of when the church began. For evangelicals, Spirit baptism is a metaphor for becoming a Christian. If the disciples became Christians on the day of Pentecost, then this metaphor would be correct. However, if the disciples became New Covenant believers prior to Pentecost, then the Pentecost event must be a subsequent giving of the Spirit. Drawing on the metaphor of baptism in Pauline theology as initiation into the church, evangelicals apply this metaphor to Luke's account of Pentecost. Howard M. Ervin offers a serious critique of that understanding.

The main text to consider is John 20:19–23. In this passage, the risen Christ appears to his disciples. After his promise to them, he breathes on them and says, "Receive the Holy Spirit." While many evangelicals see this as a Johannine Pentecost, Ervin believes that this interpretation goes beyond the context. The first issue is the time of this narrative. The disciples are hiding in the upper room following the crucifixion of Jesus. The text tells us that it is the resurrection day when Jesus appears to his followers. This event cannot be the same event as Pentecost because these two accounts are separated historically by fifty days. Secondly, in John, Jesus' promise of the coming Spirit is contingent upon Jesus' going to the Father (his ascension). Jesus repeatedly told his disciples that he must go away in order for the Spirit to come. In this upper room narrative, Jesus is physically present with his disciples when he breathes on them and tells them to receive the Holy Spirit. In Acts, the disciples are filled with the Holy Spirit because, "exalted to the right hand of God, he [Jesus] has received from the Father the promised Holy Spirit and has poured out what you now see and hear" (Acts 2:33). John's narrative and the Acts narrative are obviously not recording the same event.

Some also question whether these disciples were truly believers even after the resurrection day appearance. Ervin argues that Jesus appeared to the disciples in order to witness to his sacrificial death and resurrection. As he appeared to them, he demonstrated that he truly was the Christ. Ervin argues, "Thus he authenticated for them the fact of his bodily resurrection from the dead. Such concrete evidence was needed, since they were loath to believe the testimony of those who were first to see Him after his resurrection."[88] This appearance was necessary because true salvation is contingent upon one believing that he rose from the dead (Rom 10:9). Thus these disciples followed what became the apostolic pattern for New Covenant salvation. After faith was inspired when the disciples saw the resurrected Christ, Jesus breathed on them and said "Receive the Holy Spirit." They believed in Christ and consequently received the Spirit.

Within this account, John gives typological hints as to the nature of this giving of the Spirit. This became evident to Ervin when he realized that this event mirrors creation. As John begins his Gospel with allusions to creation, so he ends his Gospel with the new creation. Ervin says, "As God imparted life by breathing His breath into man on the day of the former creation, so also Jesus imparted new spiritual life to his followers by breathing the Holy Spirit on the day of the new creation."[89] For John, this account is describing a giving of the Spirit for the purpose of new birth. In John's Gospel, the Spirit is repeatedly coupled with the concept of life. This is the context for understanding this giving of the Spirit.

Ervin believes that when evangelicals place the disciple's salvation event at Pentecost, it poses serious theological problems. The dividing line between the Old Covenant and the New Covenant is the resurrection of Jesus Christ. As Christ died to fulfill the Old Covenant, the resurrection is the first act of creation under the New Covenant. Ervin argues that if the disciples were not saved on the resurrection day, then they would have been without a covenantal relationship with God for fifty days. Ervin argues, "Such a conclusion would violate the basic covenantal presuppositions of both the OT and NT."[90] Ervin argues that the basis for all relationship with God is covenant. It is clear in Acts and in Paul's writings that the apostolic teaching about entrance into the new covenant was expressed faith in the death and resurrection of Christ.

Ervin appeals to the story of Thomas to clearly show that the disciples fulfilled the apostolic requirements for salvation on that resurrection day. When Jesus arrives in the upper room he chastises them for their unbelief. He offers to them the nail-scarred hands and the pierced side as proof of his resurrection (John 20:20). As Thomas verifies his faith through touching his hands and side, he comes to faith and cries, "My Lord and My God" (John 20:28). This follows the apostolic pattern set by Paul when he said, "If you confess with your mouth, Jesus Christ is Lord, and believe in your heart that God raised him from the dead, you will be saved" (Rom 10:9–10). Thomas turns from unbelief to faith when he witnesses the nail-scarred hands of the risen Christ. Because of this confession, Christ breathes on the disciples and says, "Receive the Holy Spirit." It is clear now that these disciples, having expressed faith in the risen Lord, now received the Spirit from Jesus. Truly these disciples were born again by the Spirit and received eternal life just as Jesus had instructed Nicodemus.

Ervin believes that there is a categorical difference between this giving of the Spirit in John and that of Acts. He argues that John's understanding of the Spirit is ontological, while Luke's is phenomenological. When John discusses the Spirit, he does it in the context of new birth. John says that new birth is by the Spirit (John 3:5-8). New birth is an ontological change in the nature of the believer. The consequence of new birth is the beginning of the sanctifying work of the Holy Spirit. This work of the Holy Spirit brings about the fruit of the Spirit in the believer's life. Ervin says, "By its very nature, spiritual rebirth is observable only in and through the attributes of the transformed life, a life characterized by the fruits of the Spirit."[91] The life of the Spirit changes the character of the believer. The believer who abides in the vine will produce fruit as the Spirit works in his life (John 15:4). This fruit is a consequence of the ontological change in the believer. Paul tells us that the fruit of the Spirit is produced in those who walk in the Spirit (Gal. 5:16–25).

Luke's imagery of the Spirit is very different. Lukan pneumatology does not emphasize the ontological work of the Spirit. As Luke discusses the salvation event, it is always in the context of faith and repentance. Ervin says, "In the Pentecostal hermeneutic, repentance, faith, and water baptism constitute conversion and initiation into the new covenant community."[92] These are works of the Spirit theologically, but not grammatically in Luke. Luke records the phenomenological work of the Spirit. Luke is interested in what happens as a result of empowerment at Pentecost. He never mentions the work of the Spirit in the context of salvation. Instead of portraying the Spirit as the agent of salvation, Acts portrays the Spirit as the agent of functions that follow regeneration and that express witness to Jesus: inspired speech, signs and wonders, and manifestations of power. Ervin says, "The Pentecostal gift of the Holy Spirit is manifest in the charisms of the Spirit, e.g., tongues, prophecy, healings, et al."[93]

What Ervin is most concerned with is the tendency to misunderstand the unique theology and context of each of the New Testament author's emphasis on the Spirit. The biggest error evangelicals make is taking Pauline and Johannine understandings of the Spirit and applying them to Luke's narrative. Evangelicals argue that because John relates the Spirit to new birth, then the giving of the Spirit in Acts is likewise for the purpose of causing new birth. This conflating of theologies serves only to confuse the contexts and thus confuse the terms. Ervin says, "Only [through] an arbitrary harmonizing of Luke's theology of the Spirit can the Lukan gift of the Holy Spirit be equated with the Johannine new birth from above."[94] Ervin was one of the first Pentecostals to argue that Luke has his own unique pneumatology. Luke is emphasizing the Pentecostal gift of the Spirit that results in power for witness. He says, "Each reference to the Holy Spirit in Luke's Gospel and Acts must be interpreted contextually with the full recognition of the supernatural and charismatic phenomena accompanying it. To subordinate the context to an a priori theological overlay is to distort the author's intention."[95] Words have meaning in context. Ervin believes that Luke's terms must be understood in the context of Luke's writings.

For Ervin, it is clear that John tells the story of the new birth for his disciples. Luke tells the story of these new covenant believers receiving the Spirit for empowerment and witness. The birthday of the Church, that is the inaugurating day of the new covenant, is the resurrection day, not Pentecost. This means that the Pentecost event must be for a purpose other than creating New Covenant believers. Ervin believes it is clear that Luke gives the account of a subsequent giving of the Spirit that is for the purpose of empowerment with signs and wonders following.

Ervin does not deny that salvation is by the Spirit. In the context of Luke-Acts, however, the Spirit empowers those already saved. Ervin does address Paul's metaphor of being baptized into one body. A common question asked is "are not all believers 'baptized into one body' according to Paul (1 Cor. 12:13)?" To this, Ervin answers the question with a definitive "yes." But this must be understood in context. Paul uses the analogy of baptism to describe salvation. Ervin says, "That here Paul speaks of a baptism in the one Spirit into the one body, the church, argues for the initiatory significance of this baptism. It is faulty methodology, however, to read Paul's usage of this phrase into the Book of Acts, and to assert on that basis that Luke used the phrase with exactly the same meaning."[96] When Luke-Acts describes the filling of the Holy Spirit, it is always in connection with empowerment.

## A RATIONALE FOR TONGUES

The issues of the nature and function of tongues is one that every Pentecostal apologist must address. Many in the Charismatic movement consider the issue of tongues as evidence of Spirit baptism a dividing line and source of division between Charismatics and formal Pentecostals. Today, many have abandoned tongues as evidence because of such controversy. Throughout Ervin's ministry, he has always maintained that tongues are the evidence of Spirit baptism. Howard Ervin sees tongues as a vital part of the Pentecostal experience because it is a vital part of the biblical narrative. He offers a rationale for tongues that answers the questions and stays true to the text.

At the heart of the issue for Ervin is the problem of verification. When one claims to be filled with the Spirit, he questions, "How do you know?" Ervin is suspicious of vague and emotional responses to the question. The transitory nature of human emotions presents a challenge to the security of knowing one has been empowered by the Spirit. Ultimately Ervin recognizes that the reason for Spirit baptism is given in Jesus' mission statement for the experience when he says, "you will be my witnesses" (Acts 1:8). It is clear that the Pentecost experience should empower individuals to use their speech for the purpose of the gospel.

Speech is fundamental as a consequence of Spirit baptism. The Spirit empowers the believer to be a prophet and boldly proclaim the testimony of Jesus with signs and wonders that confirm the message. He says, "It should be no surprise that the human faculty preeminently used in witnessing is the power of speech."[97] Consequently, the text records that the very first act of empowerment after the Pentecostal experience was that "they all began to speak in tongues as the Spirit gave them the ability" (Acts 2:4). These tongues became a witness to all those around in Jerusalem who heard the praises of God in their own dialects. This phenomenon was the Spirit's demonstrating his "sovereign power of the human organs of communication" and thus confirming that these men and women were in fact empowered for witness.[98]

One of the most helpful insights into a rationale for tongues is Ervin's emphasis on the personhood of the Spirit. He points out that the Spirit is a person. Speech is a unique manifestation of personality. He argues that in the divine personality, speech is intrinsic. Scripture testifies to the fact that God is predominantly verbal in his dealings with man. The mode of communication between God and man is speech. God's creative activity is accomplished through speech. He says, "Speech and personhood are inseparable in the Deity."[99] Therefore the evidence that the divine personality is present is God's supernaturally communicating through yielded vessels. When someone speaks in tongues, they have surrendered their whole selves to the divine. Tongues were the unique manifestation of the Spirit's presence that signaled the new prophetic people (Acts 2:17). All other manifestations of the Spirit were present under the Old Covenant.

Ervin addresses the inevitable question, "Do I have to speak in tongues?" He believes that this question is the wrong question. He says, "It implies that the speaking in tongues precedes rather than follows the infilling with the Spirit."[100] Tongues are not what fill a person with the Spirit. Tongues are the consequence of the experience of baptism in the Spirit. When God fills a person with the Spirit, he will enable them to speak, but they do the speaking. Ervin also offers a response to those who say that they believe that they were filled with the Spirit but did not speak in tongues. The Holy Spirit does not violate the will of the individual. He does not make someone speak in tongues. If the Spirit has filled a believer, then that believer can speak, if he will. Ervin says, "If, therefore, we yield voluntarily to the Spirit's inspiration, we can speak in tongues after we have been filled with the Holy Spirit."[101] Tongues are not an ecstatic experience of uncontrollable speech. The prophetic gift of speaking by the Spirit is under the control of the person speaking. He eloquently says, "They (tongues) were the vehicle for expressing the praise and worship of men, who in full possession of all their faculties, had discovered that there are levels of communication with God that transcended the finite limitations of the purely rational. They are not, however, subrational; they are suprarational."[102]

Here it is important to discuss the nature of tongues. Ervin argues that speaking in tongues is by no means mindless babble. He says, "The tongues at Pentecost were recognizable dialects or languages. They were not the incoherent ravings of men in a trance state."[103] Because the Spirit is present and speaking, it is an actual language given by the Spirit that is unknown. Though these words are not a learned language, they are a language nonetheless. If it is truly Spirit-inspired, then the speech that comes from the Spirit will be an actual language. When one speaks in one's own native language, the words are formed in the mind and are articulated with the speech organs.[104] When one speaks in the language of the Spirit, the words come from the mind of the Spirit and are articulated by the same speech organs. This is why Paul says that he will pray with his spirit and pray with his understanding (1 Cor 14:15).

Unashamedly, Ervin appeals to the Book of Acts for the pattern of tongues as evidence. He argues, "The initial sign of the Spirit's coming, the common denominator that binds together every reference to the Pentecostal manifestations in the Book of Acts, is speech in 'other tongues as the Spirit (Himself) gave them utterance.'"[105] Ervin argues that Luke provides the sign of tongues as evidence throughout his account. These historical accounts give a unity of evidence for the experience of Spirit baptism. In each case, believers experience a filling of the Spirit that is subsequent to salvation and is evidenced by tongues (whether mentioned or implied). He argues that the confirmed evidence in the Jerusalem, Caesarean, and Ephesian Pentecosts coupled with the implied experience of the Samaritans and Paul provide an "appropriate rationale" for tongues as evidence. Thus the apostolic record establishes the pattern for Pentecost.

An additional argument for tongues as evidence is found in his distinction of the gift of tongues from tongues as a sign. Ervin argues that tongues are the sign for Spirit baptism. As Peter explains the phenomenon of the Pentecost event, he points to the tongues as the sign that Joel 2 was being fulfilled. The tongues present at the day of Pentecost were not a gift of tongues or interpretation. The gifts of the Spirit are given for the mutual edification of the body of believers in the context of the Church. Those who heard the tongues were not receiving special gifts of the Spirit to interpret the language. The disciples spoke as many languages as were present. This was a manifestation of the languages of the Spirit that served as a sign to those who heard. Tongues are the sign of the one gift of the Holy Spirit. In contrast, the gift of tongues is the ability to use the Spirit's language to speak a word of prophecy if there is a Spirit-inspired interpretation. This is something very different from what happened on the day of Pentecost and subsequent narratives. Therefore, tongues are a sign of Spirit baptism, but can be also used as a gift in the context of the Church. But tongues are not limited to the context of Church edification. The ability to speak in tongues is for the edification of the believer as well.

Many would like to offer other "evidences" of the Spirit-filled life such as spiritual gifts, holy living, and fruit of the Spirit. Ervin argues that this is going beyond the text. The most common evidence is emotional experience. Ervin warns against using emotion as a barometer for Spirit empowerment. He says, "A clear distinction must be made between the manifestation of the Holy Spirit's personality and the response of the individual experiencing the manifestation."[106] As a person encounters the Holy Spirit, they are encountering the divine Person. Emotions are very natural responses to an encounter with God. Because God is a person, those who experience his presence will have emotional responses. But each person's response to the Spirit may be very different. This provides a subjective variety of responses that may accompany an encounter with the Spirit.

Ervin points out that responses such as joy, weeping, dancing, or other emotional responses to the Spirit are the person's response, not the Spirit's manifestation. It is the personality of the individual that is visible in these demonstrations, not the personality of the Spirit that is manifesting. The only evidence given in Scripture as a pattern is speaking in tongues. All other experiences are outside of the biblical pattern. Ervin argues, "a baptism in the Spirit then without charismatic evidence is not a biblical datum. It is a theological construct dictated by subapostolic experience to extenuate the importance of the Church's life and ministry in the face of secular humanism and atheistic materialism."[107] Any attempt to make other claims as evidence is to appeal either to experience or to theological presuppositions. Ervin insists that only proper exegesis can give the pattern of evidence.

## THE PATTERN OF PENTECOST

In the book *Post Rapture Radio*, Russell Rathbun tells the story of a preacher named Pastor Nick who was sitting in a coffee shop agonizing over the Bible. The author says, "Because our tables are so close, I can hear him whisper in a sort of under-the-breath, coffee-breath tone, 'John's got the water; Jesus has got the fire. John's got the water; Jesus has got the fire.'"[108] Attempting to understand this passage, Pastor Nick creates a mercy machine that allows him to be washed and burned at the same time. Pastor Nick asks, "Where is the fire in baptism? Everybody does the water, but where is the fire?"[109] In a humorous and compelling way, Rathbun is communicating the desire to understand what Jesus meant by his baptism with fire. The Church seems to get the water right, but where is the fire? Like Pastor Nick, Ervin argues that this statement by Jesus is important for understanding the difference between water baptism and Spirit baptism. In the waters of repentance a believer joins the family of God and is born again. But Jesus baptizes with the Holy Spirit and fire. The Book of Acts is the account of this paradigm.

While many Pentecostals have abandoned the Book of Acts as a source for theological content, Ervin continues to look to Luke for theological and historical precedent. He argues that Luke provides a historical pattern in Acts for baptism in the Spirit. He says, "Each is derived from historical accounts of the various groups and individuals whose baptism in the Spirit has been recorded in the Book of Acts. Since it is only in the historical narratives of the Acts that Spirit-baptism is recorded in detail, such a formulation must depend on these records."[110] These historical accounts give a unity of evidence for the experience of Spirit baptism.

The initial pattern for Spirit baptism is derived from the message preached by John the Baptist. Jesus declared that John's baptism was a baptism for repentance. In contrast, Jesus said his baptism was in the Holy Spirit. In John's baptism the medium is water and is for the purpose of repentance. This became the norm for apostolic baptism. In Jesus' baptism the medium is the Holy Spirit and is for the purpose of empowerment. For water baptism, the apostle is the baptizer. For Spirit baptism, Jesus is the baptizer. Ervin explains it in this way: "As the baptism of John places the candidate in the medium of water, so the baptism of Jesus places the Christian in the Spirit."[111] Jesus compares the believer's baptism in water with the reality of the Pentecost experience. Just as one is immersed in water when one is saved, Jesus will immerse believers in the Spirit when he comes upon them. The grammatical symmetry created by Jesus' using the metaphor of baptism is not in order to make water baptism equal to Spirit baptism, as many evangelicals argue. The symmetry is found in the metaphor of a total immersion that is present in both events. Jesus draws on the image of being baptized to describe the reality of the Spirit's empowering presence. Pentecost places the believer in the Spirit to such a degree that it is like being immersed in the Spirit.

Paradigmatically, Jesus' baptism in the Spirit in Luke 3 sets the pattern for the baptism in the Spirit for believers who would come after him. Ervin says, "Jesus' baptism is typical of all subsequent Spirit-baptisms, not as initiatory, but for power-in-mission."[112] Luke is clear that this experience with the Holy Spirit resulted in Jesus' being "full of the Spirit" (Luke 4:1, 14). Ervin points out that for Luke, Jesus' conception by the Holy Spirit is the point of his new birth as God's son. Jesus is the Son of God ontologically by virtue of his miraculous birth by the Holy Spirit. As Jesus was born of the Spirit so too are Christians born of the Spirit through rebirth. Consequently, when Jesus approaches the waters of John's baptism he does not enter them to become a child of God, rather to fulfill all righteousness. This is the fallacy of the evangelical paradigm that links water baptism and Spirit baptism. For Jesus, his place as the child of God was linked to his birth by the Spirit. In Luke's narrative, Jesus prays after his baptism and then the Spirit descends on him to empower him for his ministry as the anointed Messiah. Ervin says, "At the beginning of His public ministry, Jesus was anointed with the Holy Spirit, thus empowering Him for this ministry of preaching, teaching and healing. Subsequently his disciples were baptized in the Holy Spirit at Pentecost for power in their lives and ministries."[113] From Jesus' experience comes the paradigm for the believer's life that is continued through the account of the Book of Acts.

## THE SEVEN PENTECOSTS

In the Book of Acts Luke gives an account of the spread of the gospel, as well as the only record of the work of the Spirit in the post-resurrection era. In a unique formulation, Howard Ervin points to seven instances in the Book of Acts that establish the pattern of Pentecost. He says, "In each subsequent recital of the experience of the believer being baptized in/filled with the Spirit, whether explicitly stated or implied, the initial manifestation of the Holy Spirit's presence and power is divinely inspired utterance, or tongues."[114] In each account, Ervin argues that this event is subsequent to salvation and is evidenced by divine speech.

## Acts 2:4 — *The Disciples' Pentecost*

It is clear that when the Book of Acts begins the discussion of Pentecost in Acts 2, these disciples were believers. Chapter 24 of Luke tells us that Jesus explained from the Scriptures all that was foretold about him. Jesus had charged them with taking this gospel that they had come to believe to the ends of the earth (Luke 24:45–53). But Jesus told them to wait in Jerusalem until they had received power from on high. Now fifty days later, these believers were waiting for the fulfillment of that promise. When that day came, the Holy Spirit was poured out on the disciples. The Spirit manifested himself by enabling the disciples to speak by the Spirit. The consequence of this filling with the Spirit was that they spoke in tongues. Immediately the disciples gave themselves to the spreading of the gospel. This Pentecost event would be recapitulated in different contexts throughout the spread of the gospel, but the common elements of subsequence and tongues would remain.

## Acts 4:31 — *The Jewish Pentecost*

This Pentecost account is one of the most unique accounts cited by Ervin and will be covered in more depth in the section on one baptism-one filling. Here we will note briefly the pattern contained in this passage, but the exegetical issues will be answered in the next section. In Ervin's understanding, the growth of the Church after Pentecost had produced in Jerusalem thousands of believers who may or may not have received the baptism in the Spirit. The account of this upper room manifestation of the Holy

Spirit provides an account of these believers filling with the Spirit. The elements of this story so parallel the Pentecost event that it is reasonable to assume that this is a recapitulation of the initial Pentecost event. Ervin says, "Then followed the second outpouring of the Holy Spirit, as at Pentecost, for (1) 'the place they were gathered together was shaken'; (2) 'they were all filled with the Holy Spirit'; and (3) they 'spoke the word of God with boldness.'"[115] Ervin explains that this was not a "refilling" of the original disciples. This was the Pentecost event for those who had joined the Church since Pentecost. Considering the large number of converts who came out of those early days, it certainly warrants an explanation about their experience of baptism in the Spirit, which may be Luke's intent by including this text.

## Acts 8:14–17 — The Samaritan Pentecost

This account gives clear evidence for the issues of subsequent and circumstantial evidence for tongues as evidence. Luke records that as Philip preached in Samaria many believed and were baptized. Though some evangelicals like James Dunn question whether these Samaritans were actually believers, this account "gives clear evidence that these Samaritan converts had become believers in the fullest sense of the word."[116] Ervin argues that this story provides the apostolic pattern for salvation. These Samaritans believed and were baptized as a result of that belief. In fact, it was so well known that these Samaritans had believed that Peter and John came down to meet them and pray that they would receive the Spirit. Ervin says, "Obviously, these two representatives of the apostolic college in Jerusalem were satisfied that these Samaritan disciples were born again in consequence of the Holy Spirit's regenerative work, accomplished through Phillip's preaching of the gospel."[117] They were not coming to pray for them because they needed to believe, but because they had believed. This story clearly shows that these were believers who had been born again and were awaiting a further filling of the Spirit. Though tongues are not mentioned in this account, it is generally accepted that this is most likely what happened.

## *Acts 8:38, 39 — The Ethiopian Eunuch's Pentecost*

The account of Philip and the Ethiopian eunuch provides another instance where subsequent Spirit baptism is implied but not specific. Philip was able to explain to the Ethiopian the saving work of Jesus Christ. As a result, the Ethiopian was baptized and then the text tells us that the Spirit took Philip away. In this text, Ervin appeals to a variant manuscript and the quotes of some of the church fathers that read, "The Spirit of the Lord fell on the eunuch, and the angel of the Lord caught away Philip."[118] In this variant we see that what happened to the eunuch followed the apostolic pattern. The Ethiopian believed, was baptized and then the Spirit fell on him. Additionally, Luke records that he went rejoicing, which is a form of verbal response to this experience. At the most this is circumstantial evidence for the pattern of Pentecost. At the least it tells us that the apostolic community believed there was a pattern and tried to preserve the normative pattern by adding this variant to the text.

## Acts 9:17 — Paul's Pentecost

In this account we find that this pattern is seen again, though not explicitly. When Jesus reveals himself to Paul on the road to Damascus, Paul becomes blind. This encounter with Jesus is life-changing for Paul. Ananias greets Paul as "brother" and tells him that he is to lay hands on Paul so that he may be healed and filled with the Spirit. Some have questioned whether Saul became a Christian on the road or when he received the Spirit. A consideration of Paul's testimony in all three accounts of this experience shows his commitment to Jesus was realized on this day. It could be argued that Saul's use of "Lord" could simply mean "sir" as a sign of respect rather than confession of submission to Jesus. Ervin argues that the use of "Lord" in this narrative is no different than other uses of "Lord" in the other eleven accounts where this word is applied to Christ.[119] Ervin argues that the pattern continues in Paul's account. He says, "He was saved, and three days later he was healed of blindness, and filled with the Holy Spirit when Ananias laid his hands upon him in the name of Jesus."[120] Consequently, after Paul is filled with the Spirit he is commissioned for his work of taking the gospel to the nations, showing that his filling with the Spirit was missional. Additionally, the fact that Paul was baptized following his conversion and Spirit baptism is further proof that the baptism in water is not the means for imparting the Holy Spirit as argued by the conversion-initiation hypothesis.

To the issue of whether Paul spoke in tongues, Ervin argues that though it is not explicitly mentioned here we do know from Paul's own testimony that he did speak in tongues. Though Paul doesn't say that he spoke in tongues on that occasion, we have no record of when he received that ability. If he did not receive it then, when did he receive it? Ervin argues, "As the record consistently bears witness, there is a causal sequence and connection between being filled with/baptized in the Holy Spirit and speaking in tongues. It is a reasonable assumption then to affirm that Paul also spoke in tongues when he received the Pentecostal gift of the Holy Spirit."[121] It can be argued that for Luke, it is sufficient to say that Paul was filled with the Spirit and thus tongues were implied. Contextually, Paul's experience continues the pattern of Pentecost.

## Acts 10:44–46 — The Roman Pentecost

In this account we see that the Pentecost event moves from those who were ethnic Jews to the Gentiles. Peter's response to the Spirit coming upon the Romans accentuates the magnitude of this event. Peter is struck by the reality that the Spirit had come upon them just as it did on those original disciples. Inherent in his words is the assumption that these Gentiles had received the same experience in the same way as the original Jewish disciples had (subsequent and evidenced by tongues). Whether separated by fifty days on Pentecost or by only minutes in this narrative, the gift of the Spirit follows the act of faith in Christ. As Peter preached about repentance and faith, these proselyte Jews embraced the message and God fulfilled his promise to give this gift to those who were "far off" (Acts 2:39). Ervin says, "Consistent then with the pattern given in the Gospel according to Luke, as Peter preached and Cornelius and his household received the message with saving faith, Jesus poured out the promised gift of the Holy Spirit upon the Roman, now Christian, household."[122]

Some use this story to assert that these Romans became Christians because of their reception of the Spirit. Ervin believes that this not only goes against the previous pattern but poses serious questions that evangelicals must address. If this reception of the Spirit for salvation was confirmed when they spoke in tongues, as Peter emphatically argues, would that create a pattern for tongues speech as a prerequisite for salvation? What role do tongues serve in the conversion? Instead, Ervin argues that this Spirit baptism event was the confirming sign that they had been given the right to become God's children. Had these Romans not received the Spirit, the Jews would have doubted their ability to be fully received into the Christian community. But because they even received the same empowerment as the disciples, it was clear that God had fully accepted the Gentiles. Ervin says, "The gift of the Holy Spirit to Cornelius and his household was God's witness to their qualification for admission to the Church by faith apart from circumcision."[123]

## *Acts 19:1–6 — The Ephesian Pentecost*

Ervin points out that this final story about the Ephesian Pentecost occurs almost twenty-five years after Pentecost. Ervin is quick to diverge from many Pentecostals who say that these disciples of John were believers in Jesus. He argues that, though they had been baptized, these disciples needed to be further taught about Jesus Christ as the Messiah (Acts 19:4). Upon hearing Paul's teaching about Jesus they were baptized in the name of Jesus.[124] Here is where Ervin finds subsequence. The text points out that they were baptized and then Paul laid hands on them and they were filled with the Spirit and spoke in tongues. Here, faith and baptism was a precondition to Paul laying hands on them to be filled with the Spirit. The time between the baptism and the laying on of hands, however brief, shows that these disciples must become believers first, then they can receive the Holy Spirit. Ervin says, "The point to be emphasized here is that Paul did not lay his hands on John's disciples to receive the Holy Spirit until after they had confessed their faith in Jesus in water-baptism."[125] Here again, the elements of subsequence and evidential tongues are consistent with the pattern.

## Conclusion

These seven narratives provide a pattern of Pentecost that in context assert that salvation is the act of repentance and faith. Spirit baptism is a subsequent work of the Spirit and is evidenced by the self-manifestation of the Spirit in speaking in tongues. This is the pattern of the early Church. It is the only narrative the Church can appeal to and therefore the only apostolic witness for the Church to follow. He concludes, "Reasoning from the experience of all the disciples in Jerusalem, Caesarea, and Ephesus (where they clearly all did speak with tongues when they were baptized in the Holy Spirit), it may be consistently argued that this was the normative pattern throughout the period covered by the New Testament."[126] Ervin provides sound exegesis and solid arguments to the Pentecostal testimony about the nature and function of Spirit baptism in the early Church.

## CONCERNING SPIRITUALS

One of the most underappreciated contributions to Pentecostal doctrine is Ervin's view of spiritual gifts. In this age of spiritual gift seminars and gifts testing, Ervin provides a refreshing and consistent view of spiritual gifts. It is often believed that each person receives one or several gifts as an endowment of the Spirit. This prevailing attitude amongst Pentecostals and Charismatics, where people receive gifts or even learn new gifts, has caused what Ervin calls a "restless quest for more and more gifts to exercise."[127] Ervin argues the present view of spiritual gifts comes from a longtime misunderstanding of the translation of "spiritual gifts" in 1 Corinthians 12. To begin with, the term gift (*charismata*) is not in the text. Of the nine so-called gifts, Paul uses the term gifts (*charismata*) only in relation to "gifts of healings." A look at the text shows that the term translated "spiritual gifts" is actually the adjective "*pneumatikon*" without a noun to modify. Ervin translates this term "spirituals." This adjective must modify a noun, so the translators have inserted the term gifts in the text. What Paul does say is that to each is given the "manifestation" of the Spirit. Ervin argues that a better understanding of Paul's opening discussion of spiritual gifts is that *pneumatikon* modifies the gifts, ministries, and workings. He says, "Taken collectively, 'gifts,' 'ministries,' and 'workings' are *manifestations* of the Holy Spirit (12:7)."[128]

Preferring the term manifestations, Ervin points out that manifestations are not permanent endowments. He says, "They are not private gifts to be exercised by the gifted at their will or whim. They are designed by the Spirit to minister to present needs in the community of believers."[129]

There is only one place where the term "gifts" is used in the text, in connection to gifts of healing. Ervin argues that these manifestations are not gifts or possessions of the Spirit-filled believer. These spirituals are manifestations of the enduring presence of the Spirit. The Spirit manifests as he will, but they are not natural abilities. There is only one gift, the Holy Spirit, but there are many manifestations.

Other passages such as Romans 12, Ephesians 4, and 1 Peter 4 do use the term "gifts." These charismata have their source in the *charis* (grace) of Jesus Christ rather than the manifestation of the Spirit. Ervin says, "In the Ephesian passage the apostles, prophets, evangelists, and pastor-teachers are individuals who have been gifted with these special *charisms*, and in turn are gifted to the Church."[130] The manifestations of the Spirit are for the edification of the Church and come as the Spirit wills. The *charisms* or *dorea* are Christ's gift to "individuals called, equipped, and 'gifted' to the church as ministers and administrators."[131] As Paul and Peter describe other gifts such as serving, giving, and hospitality, they are *charisms* that are the natural consequence of grace in the believer's life. This distinction gives honor to the offices of the Church but also keeps individuals from claiming any one particular gift of the Spirit. The practical application to this is that the Spirit is free to use whomever he chooses at any time he chooses. One cannot refuse to be used by God because they "don't have that gift." Willing vessels can be used by God for his glory and for the Church's edification.

Signs and wonders are a sign of the kingdom.[132] Ervin argues that miracles are more present in evangelism than they are in the Church. This is by design. Signs and wonders are meant to confirm the word of the gospel. They are designed to create saving faith in the individuals who see them. He says, "The messianic signs, therefore, are salvific. They cannot be divorced from the salvation context of preaching of the gospel of the kingdom with the invitation to discipleship."[133] The believing community does not need signs to confirm their faith. When unbelievers receive healing as a sign, they express faith. As Ervin says, "The faith that heals is the faith that saves, and the faith that saves is the faith that heals." [134] Ervin points out that in every case where Jesus commends someone's faith, it is a faith in Him as the Messiah that is commended. When Jesus says, "your faith has saved/healed you" it is the term *sozo*.[135]

Signs and wonders confirm the message of the gospel that is proclaimed through the empowerment of the Spirit. The same Spirit also enables Spirit-filled believers to edify the body through the manifestations of the Spirit. Signs are for the world and create faith. Gifts are for the Church and build up the body. Both are works of the Spirit but they are for different purposes. These insights into the nature of signs, wonders, and miracles help to answer the difficult questions about the role of faith and healing in the church. This contribution is much needed in this age of the Word of Faith emphasis in the Charismatic movement.

# Chapter Four

# One Baptism—
# One Filling

When Howard Ervin began to tell about his Pentecostal experience, there were few who were supporting the Pentecostal faith with sound exegesis. People began to recognize that this Princeton-trained theologian brought credibility to the Pentecostal message. Pentecostals argue that the Holy Spirit works in salvation but there is also a subsequent work of empowerment called Spirit baptism. As more Pentecostals became educated and desired to argue for their faith, the amount of academic material on Spirit baptism grew. All these works were emphasizing the empowering work of Spirit baptism and that tradition continues today.

What makes Ervin unique amongst all the scholars of the past or present on the subject of pneumatology is his unique view of "One Baptism-One Filling." Ervin is unique in that he believes the subsequent experience of Spirit baptism is a once-for-all experience. No other Pentecostal scholar holds this view. When asked about others who may hold his same view, Ervin responds, "I don't know of any."[136] Ervin's view of "One Baptism-One Filling" is unique and as such, this piece of his broader contribution to pneumatology tends to drive people away from adopting his views. It would be a shame to discount Ervin's views because this one particular view is so widely rejected, yet this is the reason this doctrine is important to the legacy of Dr. Ervin.

Though the concept of "One Baptism-One Filling" is unique, it is not inconsequential to Ervin. This doctrine is fundamental to his whole pneumatology. Ervin is convinced that the issue of re-filling is not a side issue. It is a question of correct exegesis. Ervin says, "I cannot go beyond the exegesis."[137] There is a concern in focusing on one aspect of his theology that so few agree with, when he has made so many other helpful contributions to Pentecostalism. However, when asked about this, Ervin responds, "Concerned? Yes, but unmoved. There is only one biblical solution to any question; that is the context. What does the text say? This is a case where the theology dominates, not the context."[138]

Ervin is not interested in being a maverick. He has committed his life to ministering to people from all different theological backgrounds, but Ervin truly believes that this view is essential to a correct biblical theology. Improper exegesis has consequences in one's praxis. Ervin argues that the teaching on refilling has been "a tragic theological mistake that has hindered the Pentecostal renewal."[139] Ervin has had many opportunities to minister to Pentecostals throughout his ministry. He says, "It is one of the most deadening things that have happened to Pentecost. And pastor after pastor has told me the same thing. (Their congregations are) sitting there waiting to be re-filled then they are going to take the world for Christ. Between now and then they are doing nothing. It's a deadening theology. It has absolutely no biblical support.

Exegetically it is impossible to support it." For Ervin, this issue has profound importance. This issue is important to his legacy. Howard Ervin's legacy is a commitment to exegesis that affects theology and practice.

Howard Ervin's argument for "One Baptism-One Filling" is an appeal to proper hermeneutics. As he always says, "A text without context is a pretext." This maxim is the core of his argument for one filling. Proper exegesis means understanding the terms used by a particular author in light of the author's intentions for using the terms. Terms in the New Testament are not univocal. The same is true when one approaches the Book of Acts. For Ervin, Luke uses his own terms to describe Spirit baptism. It is this principle that leads Ervin to note the relationship between the term "baptism in the Holy Spirit" and the term "filled with the Holy Spirit." Few other scholars discuss the relationship between the terms used by Luke for discussing baptism in the Holy Spirit the way Howard Ervin does. Luke never uses the term "baptized" in relation to the Spirit; he uses synonyms for that experience. Whenever a synonymous term is used in relation to the Holy Spirit, it is referring to the one experience of Pentecost (empowerment). Ervin has consistently argued that the context should determine the meaning, and not one's own experience or prior theology. He argues that proper exegesis of these texts show that his arguments are both exegetical and consistent.

## LUKE'S SYNONYMS

The first key to understanding one baptism-one filling is to note the relationship between the terms "filled with the

Spirit" and "baptized in the Spirit" in Luke's narrative. Luke never uses the term "baptism" in relation to the Holy Spirit as he records in his own words the events in the Book of Acts. This phrase is exclusive to Jesus' description of the Pentecost event. In Acts 1:5, Jesus says that they will be "baptized in the Holy Spirit," but in Acts 2:4 Luke records that they were "all filled with the Holy Spirit." Luke chooses to use other terms to communicate the phenomenon of what Jesus described as a baptism in the Holy Spirit. He notes, "In every other place where Luke made reference to the Pentecostal baptism in the Holy Spirit, he employed such phrases as the 'Holy Spirit came upon,' 'filled with the Holy Spirit,' 'received the Holy Spirit,' 'the Holy Spirit fell upon,' and 'the gift of the Holy Spirit was poured out.'"[140] If Luke chose to use the term "filled" in response to what happened on the day of Pentecost, then Luke equates "baptism" in the Holy Spirit with being "filled" with the Spirit.

It is with this understanding of the correlating relationship between filled and baptized in the Spirit that Ervin addresses being "refilled" with the Spirit. It is popular in the discussion of Spirit baptism to hear the phrase "One Baptism-Many Fillings." As the phrase suggests, believers can experience a baptism in the Holy Spirit that is followed by other subsequent fillings with the Spirit. This would imply that baptism in the Spirit describes one reality and being filled with the Spirit describes a different reality. Ervin believes that to use such a "polarization" of Luke's terms for baptism and filling would produce "a theological definition of *filling* and *baptism* that is not supported by contextual exegesis."[141] It is indeed rare to find a Pentecostal who would argue that someone needs to be baptized in the Spirit over and over. But it is not uncommon for people to seek a refilling or refreshing of the Spirit. Ervin insists that one's pneumatology must be grounded in Scripture and not in experience. There cannot be both a baptism and a filling and be true to Luke's understanding of the terms. Ervin says, "If there is one baptism in the Holy Spirit, there is one filling with the Holy Spirit."[142]

### THE STATE OF FULLNESS

The second reason Ervin believes in "One Baptism-One Filling" is because of his understanding that the Spirit baptizes believers into a state of fullness. This reality of the Spirit's empowerment is not a transitory empowerment; it is the entrance of the believer into the realm of Spirit fullness. He says, "Pentecost marked the introduction of the disciples into a state of Spirit fullness."[143] In this sense, when one is baptized in the Spirit, he or she receives the fullness of the Spirit. In the same way one enters a realm of the Spirit at conversion, there is a subsequent state of fullness in the Pentecostal experience. Ervin argues that the disciples' baptism "was an abiding endowment with power by the Holy Spirit to make them effectual witnesses for Jesus. It was not a sort of 'on again, off again, gone again' type of experience."[144] The state of fullness does not fluctuate; it has lasting consequences of empowerment for ministry. He says, "The baptism in/filling with the Holy Spirit is a once-and-for-all experience resulting in a lasting fullness."[145]

Ervin quotes the *Tyndale Bible*'s translation of Ephesians 5:18 saying, "BE FULFILLED WITH THE SPERETE."[146]

He says, "fulfilled' carries with it overtones of complete realization, or manifestation, neatly illustrated by the inversion of its members."[147] The Spirit-filled life is not only one of being filled with something, but also being complete in that fullness. The concept of completion or fullness denotes a stative concept that is not necessarily based on quantity. Though the Spirit is present in the believer, being filled with the Spirit is when one enters into the fullness of relationship with the Spirit.

He argues that the metaphor "filled with the Spirit" is a stative metaphor rather than a measurement of quantity. In his book *That Which You See and Hear*, Ervin asks the question, "How full is full?"[148] The problem with a quantitative understanding of fullness is the problem of accurately measuring such fullness. How does one know when they are full? Ervin argues that if one has been filled with the Spirit the evidence is speaking in tongues. If tongues are the initial evidence of Spirit baptism, how would someone know they have been refilled? What measurement does a person use to decide if they need refilling? This is the predicament of understanding fullness from a quantitative perspective.

Ervin addresses this problem by arguing that the term filled is not a metaphor of capacity, it is a statement of the nature of the Spirit's relationship to the believer. He says, "The term 'filled with' is a metaphor that can mislead us into erroneous extensions of the idea by the imagery it conjures up . . . the very word 'filled' conveys a static concept."[149] What he argues is that filled is not a metaphor of containing something. This would imply that being filled is a measurement of how much of the Spirit is in a person.

This would be an inappropriate metaphor because the Holy Spirit is a person of the Godhead. No one can contain the person of the Spirit. Instead, to be filled with the Spirit is an analogy for describing the Spirit work through the individual. He says, "Fullness is not how much we can contain, but how much we allow the Spirit to flow through us. That's a dynamic rather than a static image of the Spirit."[150]

Instead of a container image of fullness, he offers the analogy of a pipe.[151] If a pipe is connected to the source then that entire source is available to the pipe. The question is how open is the pipe? The problem is not how much of the Spirit one has, but how much one allows the Spirit to flow through them. Consistent with the purpose of Spirit baptism, this imagery communicates a dynamic relationship to the Spirit that makes the Spirit-filled person usable, not a possessor. This is the nature of the Spirit fullness. Fullness is not the ability to contain the Spirit but rather, "the Spirit measured in terms of the plenitude of the Spirit's manifestations through any individual life."[152] If the concept of filled were only in pure capacity terms, then one would always be in danger of lacking what is needed to be effective in ministry.

Ervin relates this concept to the incarnation. He says, "The Pentecostal visitation is, in a sense, the extension of the mystery of the incarnation, that is to say, deity clothing himself in human flesh, in human personality."[153] The other descriptions of being "clothed" and of the Spirit "coming upon" someone better conveys the reality of the Spirit-filled believer. It is the Spirit who comes to the earth, invading our human personality. It is the union of the human person with divine person, rather than a human person containing the measure of the divine Spirit. For Ervin, "Pentecost is deity in manifestation."[154] The human spirit and divine Spirit are actively living together in the fullest sense of relationship. He says, "The Holy Spirit is a living, vibrant, dynamic personality who infuses every atom, every fiber of our being with his life, his power."[155] In this sense the Spirit doesn't just fill the spirit part of our human person. The Spirit invades everything that you are until you are in perfect *perichoresis* with the Spirit.[156]

Additionally, this metaphor keeps one from viewing the Spirit as a something to get more of, instead of a Person to be in relationship with. Pentecostals tend to seek the power or anointing in a way that is separate from the person. Understanding this idea of a full relationship would negate the constant need for refilling upon every time a manifestation is needed for witness or power. To be filled with the Spirit is not to receive the additional amount of the Spirit one is lacking (for who could ever expend the amount of God one needs), but rather entering into a state of fullness or completion. Thus Ervin argues philosophically for the stative understanding of being filled with the Spirit.

### THE UNIVOCAL USE OF FILLED AND FULL

Exegetically, Ervin argues that this idea of a state of fullness is supported by the text. The grammar of the phrase that Luke uses to describe the event of Spirit baptism communicates a state of fullness. In his book *Spirit Baptism*, he argues:

> The first baptism in the Holy Spirit in the Church is described in Acts 2:1-4. As an abiding consequence

of this baptism, the disciples "were all filled with the Spirit." Here the word translated *they were filled* is an ingressive aorist tense, "commonly employed with verbs which signify a state or condition, and denote entrance into a state or condition." Pentecost marked the introduction of the disciples into the state of Spirit-fullness. The significance of both the ingressive aorist tense with the stative verb, filled, to describe the inception of the baptism in the Holy Spirit on the day of Pentecost must be underscored. . . . It was not a transitory experience that needed to be repeated but an abiding state or condition of fullness of the Spirit.[157]

Ervin's argument centers on the Greek term *eplēsthēsan* (filled) in this verse. Does this term refer to a state or an event that has only momentary consequences? Ervin argues that Luke uses this term "exclusively with states or conditions experienced by the subject of the verb."[158] Citing *A Manual Grammar of the Greek New Testament* he argues that the term "filled" in both Acts 2:4 and 4:31 are in the ingressive aorist tense. He says, "This use of the aorist tense is described thus by two New Testament scholars: 'The action signified by the aorist may be contemplated in its beginning. This use is commonly employed with verbs which signify a state or condition, *and denote entrance into that state or condition.*'"[159] Here Ervin places the weight of his view in the definition of the ingressive aorist given in this passage. He explains, "The significance of the ingressive aorist, used to describe the inception of the baptism in the Spirit on the day of Pentecost, must be underscored here. Baptized in the

Spirit by Jesus, they entered 'into that state or condition' of fullness of the Spirit. It wasn't a transitory experience that needed to be repeated. Instead it was an abiding state or condition of fullness into which they entered."[160] With the ingressive understanding of the aorist tense of the verb, Ervin has his exegetical evidence for the theological understanding of the once-for-all experience.

The main problem texts for the one filling view is the so-called re-filling texts in Acts 4. How does one understand the case of Peter, who was filled on the day of Pentecost and present in Acts 4:31 when they were "all" filled with the Spirit? Ervin believes that Peter is the perfect example of how Luke communicates the one filling. Most argue that Peter was filled at Pentecost but is refilled for the task of speaking to the Sanhedrin in 4:8 and filled again in 4:31 with the other disciples. Ervin keenly asks, "What happened to Peter's Spirit-filled experience between Acts 4:8 and Acts 4:31?"[161] In order to argue for multiple fillings one must explain what happened to Peter's Spirit-filled experience. If Peter needed multiple fillings within the span of these few days that separate these events, then what is the nature of being filled? Ervin continues to ask "Was a fullness added to fullness? (Can one be filled "fuller" then "full"?)"[162] Those who believe in re-filling must attempt to offer an explanation of the conditions that led Peter to a less than full state. Thus he argues, "Until these questions can be answered, it is futile to claim that Peter was refilled with the Holy Spirit in Acts 4:31."[163]

Instead of insisting that Peter had some sort of deficiency in his Spirit-filled experience, Ervin provides an exegetical explanation for the mystery of Acts 4. Ervin argues that Luke provides this passage precisely to demonstrate that his Spirit baptism is a lasting state of fullness. He says, "Luke had the occasion to elaborate upon the effect of the Spirit's fullness in the life of Peter."[164] Ervin believes that the context shows that the story of Peter and John's healing of the man and subsequent persecution are a consequence of that initial event of Pentecost. The power, the witness, and the signs and wonders are consequence of the one event of Pentecost in which Jesus promised power (Acts 1:8). Peter's life demonstrates the reality of Jesus' promise. Because Peter was filled with the Spirit he was able to heal the man at the gate (Acts 3:6–7) and witness before the authorities (Luke 12:12). This is Ervin's paradigm as he looks at Peter's life. For Luke, "Pentecost marked the beginning of their experience with the fullness of the Spirit."[165]

If Peter is not re-filled in Acts 4:8, then what does Luke mean when he recorded, "Peter, filled with the Spirit, said to them" (Acts 4:8)? Ervin argues that when Peter is described as "filled" with the Spirit in 4:8, it is a description of the reason Peter is able to give effective witness. His witness is no doubt a consequence of the Spirit-filling, but did it occur in that moment as an action or is Luke describing something different? Ervin argues that this was not a refilling at all; it is a description of Peter that refers to his original Pentecost experience. Ervin argues that the term filled is "regarded as adjectival (attributive)" in relation to Peter.[166] Filled is not describing a present action; it is an adjective describing Peter's state. This passage is not saying that Peter was filled with the Spirit then began to speak. It is saying that Peter is able to speak because he is Spirit-filled. To put the clause another way, Ervin translates this, "the full of the Spirit Peter said...."[167]

In this text, filled is not acting as a verb; it is an adjective. If "filled" were a verb, then this passage would describe what happened to Peter at that moment and an explanation of a re-filling would be needed. If filled is an adjective, it would describe Peter's state as a Spirit-filled believer and there would be no need for refilling. The adjectival use of this term has led some translators to translate it, "Peter, full of the Holy Spirit, said." This gives a better sense of this verse and shows the corresponding relationship of filling and fullness. He argues that rather than an action (filled), it is an adjective without an accompanying article.[168] He says, "The stative function indicates that πλησθεἰσ is used here as an arthrous attributive."[169] Consequently, the passage better reads "Peter, filled with the Spirit, answered." Here Ervin points out that the clause "filled with the Spirit" is an adjectival statement without the article "the." But the meaning is "The Spirit-filled Peter answered them."[170] In this passage, Luke was not recording that Peter was refilled in that instance. He was pointing out that Peter was already filled with the Spirit. Peter was able to give a witness before the Sanhedrin because of the fullness of the Spirit. It was the power of the Spirit supplied to Peter in Pentecost, which explains the event of the healing of the lame man, that caused him to stand before the council to give account. The larger context shows that Peter had been demonstrating the Spirit's fullness.

Ervin believes there is also no difference between being filled and being full when Luke is describing one who has received the Spirit's fullness. It is an adjectival statement about the person. This is consistent with his view of fullness as a state. He believes that Luke explains the prophetic utterance as a consequence of the speaker's fullness. Luke's use of the term *plero* (full) is used to describe Jesus, the seven deacons, Stephen, and Barnabas. He argues, "the noun by its very nature is stative, and underscores the fact that an abiding fullness of the Spirit was the normative result of being baptized in the Holy Spirit."[171] Because one is baptized in the Spirit they are full.

This is best shown in the life of Jesus. Luke records, "Jesus, full of the Holy Spirit, returned from the Jordan" (Luke 4:1). Jesus had entered into the state of fullness at his baptism in the Jordan. Was there additional empowerment needed from the time of his baptism to his journey to the wilderness or is this passage describing the result of his baptism? Likewise as the deacons are being chosen, the church is looking for those who were full of the Holy Spirit. There is nothing to indicate that the ones chosen had only a transitory empowerment.

**THE SO-CALLED REFILLED TEXTS**

The main texts in Acts used by many to argue for multiple fillings are Acts 4:8 and Acts 4:31. It is Ervin's contention that all of these events describe something other than a doctrine of multiple fillings. This is where the doctrine of "One Baptism-One Filling" rises and falls. It is Ervin's ability to make his arguments in these passages that makes his argument unique to Pentecostal scholarship.

At the heart of the argument is his understanding of Acts 4:31. This is the most controversial and truly unique

Pentecostal position that Ervin argues. James Dunn is highly critical of his interpretation. He says, "His treatment of 4.31 involves some rather unnatural and tortuous exegesis which cannot be accepted."[172] Ervin labels this passage the "Jewish Pentecost."[173] Traditionally, Pentecostals interpret this event as an additional filling with the Spirit. The presence of Peter and John at this event where "they were all filled with the Holy Spirit and spoke the word of God with boldness" is used to argue for additional fillings (Acts 4:31). Ervin disagrees with this based on the context.

First, he makes the case that the exact same terms used in 2:4 are used in 4:31. The phrase "they were all filled" (*epl-ēsthēsan pantes*) is the same phrase in both passages. This presents a grammatical symmetry between the two events. In both instances they were all filled. By parity of reasoning, if the Acts 2:4 event was what Jesus describes as a baptism in the Spirit, then Acts 4:31 was a repetition of a Pentecost type of event. Whatever it meant to Luke in Acts 2:4, it must also have meant the same in Acts 4:31.

Secondly, there is a phenomenological symmetry between the two events. In Acts 2:4, there were visible signs of God's presence such as tongues of fire and the sound of mighty wind. In Acts 4:31, the place where they were gathered was shaken. Both represent a theophany of God's presence that shakes the created order.

There is also symmetry in the results of this filling experience. In 2:4, they were all filled and spoke in other tongues. In 4:31, they all were filled and spoke the word of God with boldness. The result of each of these fillings was inspired speech. In 2:4 they were empowered to witness, in 4:31 they were empowered to speak boldly. Ervin argues, "Notice, the results of this filling, ie. baptism, is the same in both Acts 2:4 and 4:31. The immediate response is speech."[174] There is a definite symmetry between the events. If this is a Pentecost type event, then who was filled? Were not Peter and John present? Would they not also be part of the "all"?

Ervin answers the dilemma posed in Acts 4:31 based on the context of the story. His explanation shows a consistent understanding of terminology and evidence. First he argues that the "house" in 2:4 and the "place" in 4:31 are not the same terms. He argues that the number of people in the place is not restricted to a certain number. Because of this it certainly could include more than just the original 120. He argues that the next verse, 4:32, indicates that there were many or even multitudes in the place where they gathered.[175] Ervin believes that the multitudes who are the subject of the Spirit baptism episode are those new converts who were made since Pentecost. But could there be a prayer meeting that could accommodate the thousands who had been added to the church? Ervin argues that for the Jewish people, the places of prayer were often not confined to rooms or synagogues, but were also wide open places. He says, "The customary *topos proseuches*, 'place of prayer,' of the Jews may well have supplied the pattern for such a Christian gathering place apart from the Temple and the synagogues of Jerusalem."[176] Those who had heard the word and were converted were gathered together to pray. Consequently, Peter's prayer for boldness resulted in these converts being filled with the Spirit. With the growing number of converts reaching 5,000 by Acts 4:4, it is certainly possible that many had not yet received baptism in the Spirit. In Acts 4:31, Peter's words on Pentecost were realized. The converts from the Pentecost sermon and the daily growth of the church had now been granted the same gift as those original 120 disciples.

But doesn't the "all" refer to those disciples who were previously filled as well? Again the "all were filled" can either refer to the action happening at that time or the collective state of them all. Were they all re-filled or did the whole company reach fullness? The former would include a refilling of the disciples; the latter would indicate an advance of the rest of the company to the level of those original disciples. The context determines who the "all" is referring to. The context is a prayer for boldness that all the believers would speak and do signs and wonders (Acts 4:29–30). This phenomenology is the same as the Pentecost event. It could be rendered, "And the place was shaken and they all (including the converts) were (now at the same state) filled with the Spirit and spoke boldly (because of it)." The "all" (*pantes*) must refer to those who were not already filled, which considering the size of the crowd, could be a large number. The result of this filling of the new converts meant that the whole company, which included Peter and John, were now all filled with the Holy Spirit. Not one person of the church at that time was excluded. Ervin says, "The Spirit-filled state 'has now been realized' by all the Christians." [177]

Ervin answers the question of the additional fillings of Acts 4:8 (Peter) and 13:9 (Paul) grammatically. He says, "I conclude, therefore, that the use of the passive participle πλησθείσ in Acts 4:8 and 13:9 describes an antecedent state or condition of Spirit fullness."[178] He argues that the uses of filled (*plestheis*) are adjectival. This means that the filling of Peter and Paul was not the cause for the inspiration for their speech. A Spirit-filled Peter and Paul spoke because of this empowerment. He translates Acts 4:8 as "then Peter, full of the Holy Spirit, answered them."[179] Here the phrase, full of the Spirit, is adjectivally describing Peter, not an event. He says, "The attributive adjective stresses some quality or attribute of the noun it modifies. Freely translated, the clause reads, 'full-of-the-Spirit Peter said,' which equals 'Spirit-filled Peter said.'"[180] He notes that the *Good News for Modern Man* translation picks up this very point when it translates "Peter *full* of the Holy Spirit."[181] In both cases Acts 4:8 and 13:9, Luke is communicating that their previous fillings were the reason they are speaking. It is the Spirit's presence that empowers them to speak prophetically.

It has been suggested that the Spirit filled Peter for the immediate need of speaking to the Sanhedrin. Ervin believes that "the sudden inspiration of the Spirit in the face of imminent crises may just as well be attributed to the indwelling presence of the Spirit. If Peter is in need of refilling within such a short period of time, then what exactly is the lasting effect of Spirit baptism? In order to argue for refilling, one must provide reason why Peter loses his fullness quickly. Otherwise, the filling must only be a momentary filling for the specific immediate need, which some have suggested. If it is only momentary, then how true is Jesus' promise of power? And what does this look like practically? This would suggest that the Spirit must fill a person every time they are to give verbal witness for Christ. For Ervin the clearer and more logical answer is that Spirit baptism is a once-for-all experience where one enters into a state of the Spirit's fullness. This is what Jesus promises. It is a lasting empowerment. It a state of fullness so dramatic that Luke characterizes individuals as "filled" or "full" of the Spirit.

**THE FUNCTIONAL GIFT**

The argument for one baptism and one filling is also an argument for the purpose of the Spirit baptism. There is a symmetry of responses to being filled with the Spirit that suggests that these "refilling" passages are either describing initial fillings or the testimony of Spirit-filled people. Ervin argues that for Luke, the purpose of Spirit baptism is phenomenological. Jesus proclaims, "But you will receive power when the Holy Spirit comes on you and you will be my witnesses" (Acts 1:8). Evangelical scholars argue that Spirit baptism is the conversion experience. Ervin maintains what would be considered the classical Pentecostal position. He says, "It is a consensus of the classical Pentecostal view that the baptism in the Holy Spirit (Acts 2:4) is *subsequent* to conversion and the new birth. This argues for two clearly distinguishable actions of the Holy Spirit in the life and experience of the believer."[182] Ervin believes that this is truly Luke's purpose in his narrative. He also argues that this same understanding reaches all the way back to the Old Testament prophets. He says, "The coming of the Spirit 'upon' the OT prophet signified His consecration and empowerment to fulfill the prophetic office to which He had been called. . . . Jesus in appropriating the words of the OT prophet for himself, identified His baptism in the Spirit as empowerment for a prophetic ministry."[183] The work of

Pentecost initiates believers into the role of becoming prophetic people who proclaim God's kingdom to the whole earth. If there is a transitory nature to this empowerment, how can there be any assurance that one is ready in season and out of season for this task? A never-ending mission must come with never-ending power.

Ervin argues against a transitory understanding of this empowerment by the Spirit by relating it to salvation. He says, "The transitory nature of human emotions, however, does not argue for transitory and repeated fillings with the Holy Spirit. . . . Were this possible, then one could by the same logic argue that the new birth is also a transitory and repetitive experience."[184] This is Ervin's pastoral concern with multiple fillings. He is cautious of those who go from experience to experience in hopes that the next filling will finally make them ready for ministry. The purpose of Spirit baptism is evangelism. Believers must be confident in the Spirit's lasting fullness to be ready to share the gospel at all times. Ervin says, "The consequences of this refilling (emphasis) are so unfortunate that it has hindered evangelism."[185] An emphasis on refilling has allowed the Church an excuse not to do the work they should have been empowered to do. The idea of re-filling is not only contrary to the purpose of Spirit baptism but also cannot be supported with the biblical text. Too often people are hesitant to be witnesses because of their feelings of inadequacy. Many seek for new experiences hoping to feel qualified to be witnesses. But Ervin argues, "Parity between the categories of human emotions and Spirit-fullness cannot be demonstrated."[186] Feelings are not a good barometer of how "full" someone is any more than they inform someone of how "saved" they are. As in salvation, we must trust in the promise that we have been filled with the Spirit and are empowered to be a witness whether we feel like it or not. Otherwise, the work of spreading the gospel will be subject to our ever-changing emotions and the task will never be done. Our experience of Pentecost is in vain if we are insecure about the reliability of the empowerment of that experience.

## CONCLUSION

Howard Ervin is unique in his emphasis on one baptism-one filling. No other Pentecostal scholar has insisted on this view. The practice of refilling by Pentecostal churches has not only exegetical and theological problems, but it also has practical ramifications for the effectiveness of Spirit-filled believers. Too often Pentecostals have bowed at the altar of experiential Christianity, rather than critically look at the text. As many believers long for experiences with the Spirit, they can easily become distracted from the reason that they were baptized in the Spirit in the first place. Ervin's arguments against refilling are not only sound exegetically, but provides a consistent and pastoral understanding of Spirit baptism.

### *A Consistent View*

When Ervin approaches Luke-Acts, he endeavors to let Luke define his own terms. This is the strength of Ervin's view of Spirit baptism. Luke uses synonyms to describe the one event of what Jesus called a baptism in the Holy Spirit. Anywhere Luke uses these terms he is describing this one event. Ervin alone remains consistent to this premise. All other scholars make these terms mean something different in order to accommodate the refilling view of the texts. However, Ervin stays consistent in his belief that when Luke uses the term filled with the Spirit, he means baptized in the Spirit. Ervin will even risk being unpopular in order to stay true to the text. Ervin's first allegiance is to the text. He is committed to experience as long as it is based on a sound reading of the text. His view of re-fillings is not based on experience. It is always based on Scripture and the contextual principles that guide its interpretation.

## A Pastoral View

Howard Ervin spent twenty years in the pastorate and another twenty years traveling and speaking on the Holy Spirit. He is aware of the struggles that believers face on a daily basis. Dr. Ervin is concerned that believers do not live in the power given to them by the Spirit. Ervin's great concern with re-filling is based on his experience in praying for hundreds of Pentecostals. He says, "It has been our personal observation that this teaching of initial filling with subsequent re-fillings with the Holy Spirit has been a source of paralysis to the life and witness of many Spirit-filled Christians."[187]

Dr. Ervin is not only concerned for proper exegesis. He is concerned with proper praxis. He believes that the baptism in the Holy Spirit is truly power for witness. God not only gives power, but this power is more than enough for the believer to be an effective witness. Many people have received the Spirit but have not lived in the power that

He provides. Because an encounter with the Spirit carries a real emotional element, many people look only to those emotional encounters to feel full of the Spirit. But Ervin argues that empowerment is not about emotion. He says, "My position stands or falls on the exegesis, not the emotion."[188] Spirit baptism is about becoming a living witness. He says, "The real tragedy is this; that these very people have been endued with power, but refuse to believe it, or act upon it, because they have been taught otherwise. So they sit forlornly by rather than moving obediently in Spirit-filled witness to a lost humanity, trusting the Spirit to manifest Himself sovereignly and charismatically whenever they bear witness to Jesus as Savior and Lord."[189]

When believers are baptized in the Spirit to be a witness for Christ, they must trust that God has truly given them the power to be what he asked them to be. Ervin is concerned that believers are looking to their next experience to truly be filled. However, situations in life will always convince us that we have dropped below the level of fullness. In this culture where believers are quick to receive and slow to give, the problem is not supply, but action. Rather than pointing the Church to further fillings with the Spirit, Ervin urges the Church to get out there and do something with what they have.

Secondly, there is a pastoral advantage to his view. Ministers deal with the daily fluctuation of life in the ministry. The trials of a minister can be great. If a minister is always worried about having a new experience every time they need to minister to people, then they will live in a constant state of unrest. Conversely, if a minister knows that they have entered a state of fullness that they can rely on, then ministers can be confident that God will be with them as they step out in faith. If the idea of re-fillings is true, then ministers and believers alike can question their readiness for evangelism if they have not been refilled recently. Ervin believes that the baptism in the Spirit is a state of fullness where the Spirit manifests himself through the believer for the power to preach the kingdom of God. This fullness is always available and is not dependant on human emotion. Pastors can encourage their flocks to do the work they have been empowered to do rather than spending their time trying to redo the same experiences over and over. The task is great, but God has promised power from on high to accomplish the great commission. Now we must live in and act upon this power to reach the lost.

Chapter Five

Answering
# His Critics

In the history of Pentecostalism there has been much debate between Pentecostals and non-Pentecostals about Spirit baptism. The debate centers on the issues of subsequence, tongues, purpose, and gifts of the Spirit. There also has been debate between Charismatics and Pentecostals on their own differences. A good example of this debate is the recent book *Perspectives on Spirit Baptism: Five Views*.[190] This book presents the current debate about the ontological and phenomenological understandings of Spirit baptism from five differing points of view. With the diversity of beliefs about Pentecost today, Howard Ervin has consistently argued for the classical Pentecostal understanding of Spirit baptism.

Because Ervin's view of one filling is so unique, those who have addressed his pneumatology have engaged this topic the most. Ervin's pneumatology is argued from the text. Because his views are consistent and integrated, an adequate defense of the criticisms against one filling will answer most of the critics' questions about his pneumatology. This section will outline the arguments against this view from a theological and exegetical viewpoint. The rebuttal arguments will be limited to those who have critiqued him. Outside of his rebuttal to James Dunn, Ervin did not engage his critics. This section will be an analysis of their critiques and what this author believes would be his response.

The evangelical side will be represented by Ervin's contemporaries such as Anthony Hoekema and James D. G. Dunn. The modern evangelicals and Charismatics will be represented by Larry Hart, Max Turner, and Craig Keener. The Pentecostals will be represented by Stanley Horton and Roger Stronstad. All these who represent their respective movements disagree with Ervin's premise of one filling. This chapter is an examination of the actual arguments against One Baptism-One Filling in order to see if these scholars have adequately argued against his views. The outcome will show that Ervin's views are still valid, consistent, and useful in the discussion of Pentecost today.

## CONTEMPORARIES RESPOND

One approach to being filled with the Spirit is the evangelical view that Spirit baptism is conversion. This view assumes from Paul's teaching that when you become a Christian you receive the Holy Spirit. Therefore, when the believers in the Book of Acts receive the Holy Spirit, they become Christians. But this view also necessitates that evangelicals hold to the idea that there is one baptism (conversion) in the Holy Spirit but there can be many fillings. The fillings take all sorts of forms from empowerment, to immediate speech inspiration, to manifestations of good character and fruits of the Spirit. All such views, though rejecting a subsequent work of

Spirit baptism, do affirm a subsequent working of the Holy Spirit after conversion. Additionally, Pentecostals reacted to Ervin's view of one baptism-one filling. Pentecostals commonly argued there is one baptism in the Spirit and many fillings. A look at Ervin's contemporaries will show the responses made to Ervin's most unique view.

## *Anthony Hoekema*

In 1970, New Testament scholar Anthony Hoekema wrote his work analyzing the Pentecostal understanding of Spirit baptism. Whereas Ervin would argue that baptism and filling are synonyms, evangelicals like Anthony Hoekema would disagree. Rejecting the Pentecostal view of subsequence, Hoekema says, "If you are true believers you don't need to seek a baptism in the Spirit; you have, in fact, already been baptized in the Spirit."[191] Hoekema is quick to remove any Pentecostal second work from the equation by equating Spirit baptism to conversion. He believes that though all are baptized in the Spirit, believers still need to be filled with the Spirit. He says, "According to the New Testament teaching, all believers have the Spirit dwelling within them, but not all believers continue to be filled with the Spirit."[192] What Hoekema fails to do is see the grammatical correlation of baptism in the Spirit with being filled with the Spirit. As Ervin points out, Luke used the term filled as a synonym for what Jesus calls baptism in the Spirit. Additionally, the very idea of an additional work of the Spirit is rejected, yet he argues for the importance of a continual work of the Spirit in the believer's life.

Many evangelicals are critical of Pentecostals for their emphasis on experience to prove their theology. Because of this, it is surprising that Hoekema would appeal to experience for his view of repeated fillings. He says, "The fact that, though Christians receive the Spirit at the time of conversion, they do not necessarily remain filled with the Spirit is confirmed by our experience. Believers may drift away from God, may grieve the Spirit, may become proud, quarrelsome, loveless or self-indulgent. In such instances they will need once again to recover the fullness of the Spirit which they had when they were converted."[193] The assumptions of this view are twofold. (1) Baptism/filled with the Spirit is related to one's conduct or closeness to God and not empowerment for mission. (2) One's baptism must be maintained or we can fall below fullness and must be refilled.

This view is an example of a failure to read Luke in context. Ervin argues that if one does not recognize the relationship between baptism in and filling with the Spirit for Luke, one can be both baptized and not full of the Spirit. There is an inconsistency in this view. If baptism in the Spirit is salvation and Luke uses the term "filled" for baptism in the Spirit, what is the state of someone who needs to be re-filled? Are they less than saved? However, if baptism is something different than filling, is Luke's terminology taken seriously? Ervin not only insists that Spirit baptism for Luke is not salvation, but that these terms cannot be separated.

Hoekema does offer an exegetical response to these beliefs. He identifies three different ways that "filled with the Spirit" is used. The first understanding is described by Hoekema as a momentary empowerment. He says, "Sometimes being filled with the Spirit is a momentary experience which qualifies one for a specific task he is about to perform."[194] He identifies this momentary action in Acts 4:8, 4:31, and in 2:4. Hoekema would agree with many Pentecostals about the purpose of these fillings. He says, "The filling with the Spirit spoken of here was a specific bestowal of the power of the Spirit on Peter, enabling him to speak boldly about the Christ in whose name this man had been healed."[195] This filling is momentary and for the purpose of empowerment.

It is obvious that Hoekema would not consider that these baptisms in the Spirit are conversion experiences. It is here that he concludes, "To be filled with the Spirit, therefore, in the light of these passages, is not something that happens only once for all; it may be repeated."[196] Because of Acts 4:8 and 4:31, he concludes, not from exegesis, but from reasoning that these were subsequent fillings for the purpose of empowering for those who had already been filled. Again, there is no mention to his original premise that baptism in the Spirit is what makes one a Christian. If Acts 2:4 is a "momentary experience," then what is the nature of their born again experience? Were they saved only momentarily? This is the result of a failure to connect the two terms. This is where Ervin stands as a faithful witness to good exegesis of Luke-Acts. Ervin is consistent when he says, "The baptism in the Holy Spirit is, for Luke at least, synonymous with being filled with the Spirit. Jesus, speaking prophetically of the Pentecostal baptism in the Spirit said, 'you shall be baptized in the Holy Spirit.'" Luke, in recording the phenomenology of the event, wrote, "they were all filled with the Spirit."[197]

Ervin does agree with Hoekema and other evangelicals that Paul does refer to a baptism in the Spirit that is in relation to the work of the Spirit in salvation. Ervin understands the exegetical arguments for the Pauline understanding of this term. But, he does argue that this is foreign to the Lukan understanding of Spirit baptism. He says, "If Paul did equate 'baptism in the Spirit' in 1 Cor. 12:13 with regeneration, can it be argued from this fact that the same phrase means the same thing in the Gospels and in the Book of Acts?"[198] The refilling texts in question are not Paul's texts, they are Luke's texts. When Luke uses the term baptism in the Spirit he is referring to the empowering work of the Spirit. Ervin contends, "1 Cor. 12:13 stresses two aspects of the Christian's relationship to the Holy Spirit. To be 'baptized in the Spirit' is to be placed in the sphere of the Holy Spirit, that is at conversion; while 'being given to drink of the Spirit' places the Spirit's fullness within the believer."[199] So, though Paul uses the phrase baptized into one Spirit for conversion, he is also aware of an additional dimension of the Spirit.

In addition to an empowerment understanding of the term filled, Hoekema also argues for the term filled as a description of the character of certain people. For these individuals, he says, "Being filled with the Spirit is not just a momentary endowment for a specific purpose, but a permanent characteristic of a person's life."[200] The previous use was functional, this filling is ontological. Hoekema finds examples of this in the fullness of Jesus, Stephen, and the seven deacons. What Hoekema is arguing is that when someone is described as "full," it is a statement about their character. It is not a momentary empowerment; it is a state. For evangelicals, all who are converted are baptized/filled.

It would be foolish to distinguish those who were full from those who weren't. If there are some who are not characterized as full of the Spirit, then they are not Christians and therefore disqualified from consideration. Ervin would argue that the reason that the distinction was made is because not everyone is "filled with the Spirit." The requirements given were that those who served in leadership would need to have been filled with the Spirit. Stephen would be described as full because he had been filled. His baptism in the Spirit qualified him for the position of leadership. Therefore he was not a man of particular piety or character other than he was one who had been filled with the Spirit. Since everyone is not filled automatically at conversion, there will naturally be those who were filled and those who were not

The final use of filled is the continual filling referenced in Acts 13:52 and Ephesians 5:18. Hoekema says, "Here the tense of the verb is present, meaning that we must be continually filled with the Spirit."[201] One cannot "claim to have received this filling once and for all."[202] This continual filling is related to a holy, God-centered life. This understanding is foreign to a Lukan view of Spirit-filled life. He concludes the chapter with this: "Believers do not need to seek a post-conversion 'baptism in the Spirit,' but they do need to be continually filled with the Spirit who dwells in them."[203] Hoekema places in the metaphor of being Spirit-filled not only empowerment, but fruit of the Spirit and a person's relationship with God. Baptism in the Holy Spirit, on the other hand, is salvation, not empowerment. It is a one-time event and permanent because it is the sealing of the Holy Spirit. Baptism in the Spirit is not the filling of the Spirit. The filling of the Spirit is a secondary and continual work of the Spirit where one is empowered, characterized, or filled with the Spirit's fruits. Ervin would argue that any attempt to make a distinction between baptism and filling is artificial and an incomplete understanding of Luke's theology. Pentecostals have continued to insist that evangelicals let Luke speak for himself and not synthesize Luke's views of Spirit baptism with Paul's use of the terms baptized and filled.

## *James D.G. Dunn*

James Dunn's work on the Holy Spirit not only engages Pentecostals, but Ervin in particular. James Dunn goes to great lengths to show that Pentecost is the birthday of the Church. Though Ervin deals with Dunn's presuppositions in detail in his work *Conversion-Initiation and Baptism in the Holy Spirit*, only his view of many fillings will be analyzed here. Dunn says, "One does not enter the new age or the Christian life more than once, but one may be empowered by or filled with the Spirit many times."[204] Dunn argues that Spirit baptism is conversion. He argues, "To become a Christian, in short, is to receive the Spirit of Christ, the Holy Spirit. What the Pentecostal attempts to separate into two works of God is in fact one single divine act."[205]

The Spirit is given to the Christian at conversion, but what of the "baptism" Jesus promised? Dunn says, "For Luke there are only two baptisms; water baptism and Spirit-baptism (Luke 3:16; Acts 1:5; 11:16). In the former, 'baptism' means only the rite of immersion and nothing more; in the latter, it means only the (manifest) giving of the Spirit and nothing more."[206] God gives one the Spirit when they believe and not in the rite of baptism. But what is important for Dunn is that the giving of the Spirit is only linked to conversion. He says, "Luke knows of no other coming of the Spirit than that described in these phrases. . . . In every one of the 23 occurrences which the Pentecostals claim for his second distinctive work, Luke is describing what is for him the first coming of the Spirit."[207] Here Dunn recognizes that Spirit baptism has many phrases that describe the same experience. He says they are "equivalent ways of describing the same coming of the Spirit."[208] While Dunn and Ervin would agree on this point, they would disagree on the nature of these events. Dunn describes this as salvation, while Ervin argues for an empowerment experience. This cannot be discussed at length, but it shows the presuppositions that each tradition brings to the text. What matters is what Luke means by these events.

Dunn recognizes that all these "givings" (he chooses not to call them baptisms or fillings) relate to the same event of salvation in every case. He says, "For him (Luke) there is only one coming of the Spirit which he describes in various ways."[209] He violates his own principle by saying that "one may be empowered by or filled with the Spirit many times."[210] While he connects the various phrases used by Luke, one would think he would reject totally any additional givings of the Spirit for any other reason such as multiple fillings. Instead, Dunn takes on Ervin's belief in one baptism-one filling by critiquing his exegesis of Acts 4 by calling it, "rather unnatural and tortuous exegesis which cannot be accepted."[211] But if Dunn believes that all givings of the Spirit in Acts are givings for salvation, then why would he critique Ervin's treatment of 4:31? He includes the phrase used in Acts 2:4 and 4:31 in the "23" terms used for a salvation giving of the Spirit. But he diverts from his premise by admitting that Acts 4:8 and 4:31 would be "the sudden inspiration and empowering of the Spirit which Jesus had promised for the special occasion . . . and which would not last beyond the hour of need."[212]

Dunn's recognition of Luke's terms describing the same event of conversion (or giving of the Spirit) appears to be inconsistent with his view of many fillings. Straying from his view of Pentecost as the birthday of the Church, he admits that these fillings were in fact for the purpose of empowerment. He says, "Since Luke goes on to describe a further filling with the Spirit in 4.31 he obviously felt no inconsistency between these descriptions and the previous account of the Pentecostal filling (2.4)."[213] Again he is changing the meaning of Pentecost as he deals with the additional filling passages. He says of 4:31, "For Peter, presumably, this was the third time he had been filled with the Spirit."[214] Can one accept this view of three fillings for Peter when, as Dunn says, Luke knows of "only one giving of the Spirit"?[215] He cannot claim that all of Luke's terms describe the one giving of the Spirit for salvation and at the same time say that Peter had been filled three times. He must either create the possibility of a subsequent giving of the Spirit or agree with Ervin that these are not re-givings of the Spirit. The text of 4:31 is consistently a problem text for all who approach it.

## Stanley M. Horton

Evangelicals were not the only ones forced to deal with these passages. Pentecostals also dealt with 4:8 and 4:31.

Stanley Horton, an Assembly of God scholar and contemporary of Howard Ervin, wrote his book *What the Bible Says about the Holy Spirit* in 1976.[216] Revered as one of the early Pentecostal scholars, the Assemblies of God looked to Horton to articulate their beliefs. Horton was familiar with Ervin and interacted with him in his discussions on the refilling passages. Horton insists that new fillings are necessary for the Christian life. These new fillings are important for the new challenges given to the Church. In reference to Acts 4:8, Horton says, "This time, as Peter stood up he was filled anew by the Spirit and gave an answer that proclaimed the truth and glorified Jesus."[217] Horton contends that the verb form in 4:8 and 4:31 argues for fresh fillings. He says, "the form of the verb indicates a new special filling."[218] Though he makes his point in opposition to Ervin, Horton does not expand on the actual exegesis of this argument. This shows the nature of most Pentecostal scholarship of this era. Horton was concerned with the readability of his book by the common believer and assumed, rather than explained, the scholarship behind the argument. Ervin in contrast expounded on his exegesis at length in his books. Parenthetically this shows how Ervin was ahead of his time in the Pentecostal world.

Horton specifically mentions Ervin's view of Acts 4:8. He says, "Ervin supposes this could not be because Peter was already filled and full. But the idea is not that he had lost anything from the previous fillings."[219] Horton answers Ervin's question by arguing that this filling was an expansion of his fullness for the current situation. Horton essentially argues that Peter had his capacity for fullness expanded.

It would be helpful for Horton to explain exactly what in this text brings him to this conclusion. He argues that Acts 4:31 was also a special filling because of the verb form, but no explanation for why the verb form in 4:31 is the same in 2:4. Horton writes, "The Greek indicates again a new, fresh filling of the Spirit. Some writers (Ervin) contend that only the new people (the 5,000 mentioned in 4:4) were filled at this time. But the Greek does not uphold this. All the believers, including the apostles, received this fresh filling to meet the continued need and the pressures upon them. New, fresh fillings of the Holy Spirit are part of God's wonderful provision for all believers."[220]

Horton fails to explain how the Greek rules out Ervin's view. Does the Greek indicate that for the disciples it is a refilling and for the converts it is an initial filling? The Greek does not indicate the type of filling that took place anymore than it tells us who the people are who received it. The context must explain who the people were and what happened. Ervin argues that the context includes those five thousand believers that entered the church in Acts 4:4. Horton's argument does not give an exegetical explanation but it does reflect the theological paradigm for interpreting these passages as fresh fillings. Horton says, "Fresh fillings, fresh anointings, fresh moves of the Spirit, new manifestations of the hand or power of God are always available in the time of need."[221]

It is the emphasis on new experiences with the Holy Spirit that drives many Pentecostals to a view of many fillings. When asked why Pentecostals did not accept his view, Ervin speculated, "The problem was that I was dealing with it hermeneutically and exegetically, but the whole emphasis was on the experience. So they were not ready to deal with it exegetically."[222] Horton and other Pentecostals insist on additional fillings because of their own experience. Ervin insists that those who believe in re-filling should be able to argue from Scripture and not experience. Without more information and detailed exegesis it is a challenge to understand how Horton disagrees with Ervin other than by experience.

### MODERN CRITICS

The explosion of scholarship in the modern era has produced some fine New Testament theologians. Among them are a number of scholars who have done their studies on Luke-Acts. This era of scholarship has produced profound developments in the area of pneumatology. Since the 1980s, scholars like Roger Stronstad, Max Turner, James Shelton, and others have done much to add to academia's understanding of Luke-Acts.

### *Roger Stronstad*

In 1984, Roger Stronstad, a Pentecostal, entered the debate with his work *The Charismatic Theology of St. Luke*.[223] Stronstad produced a pivotal explanation of the unique theology of Luke-Acts. He argued that Luke was an independent theologian and that Luke's use of the Holy Spirit was linked to empowerment. He also pioneered the recognition of the link between Luke's terms and the Septuagint. This work gave Pentecostals solid exegetical and theological backing for subsequence and empowerment. Stronstad argues that the uses of the phrases in Luke-Acts are all part of the prophetic heritage of the Old Testament. With careful exegesis he identifies the tenses of the verbs and phenomenon that occur in all instances of "filled with the Spirit." He concludes that there are nine uses of this phrase in Luke-Acts. Among those instances are Acts 2:4, 4:8, and 4:31.

He engages Ervin's view from an exegetical standpoint. He is one of the few who would argue specifically against his exegesis with detailed exegesis of his own. His conclusions against Ervin are that "being filled with the Spirit is not a once-for-all experience."[224] He says, "Howard M. Ervin challenges this interpretation. Since the aorist participle usually describes an action which precedes the main verb, he concludes that Luke's description of Peter (Acts 4:8) and Paul (Acts 13:9) point to their previous fillings by the Spirit."[225] In rebuttal, Stronstad argues that the term "filled" is linked to the term "said" and is a contemporary experience rather than pointing to Peter's past experience. He argues, "The aorist participle describes an action which is contemporaneous with and not prior to, the main verb."[226]

He argues that the aorist tense carries a punctiliar action which is event-oriented. This would make the filled for Peter in 4:8 a present action. Ervin argues that this aorist is ingressive, which would indicate a state. Stronstad argues that it is punctiliar and not ingressive, but if it were ingressive, the evidence would support Ervin. He says, "If Luke's aorists are ingressive aorists, then on the day of Pentecost, the disciples would have entered into a permanent and continuous state of being filled."[227] Stronstad recognizes that if it can be proven that filled describes a state, then the Greek could support this view. But he does not prove one argument over the other; he simply concludes that "obviously this did not happen."²²⁸ Ervin argues that filled is ingressive which denotes a state or condition of being filled. Stronstad believes that the verb carries the normal function. He is not able to argue that the verb in 2:4 is not ingressive. He argues that it cannot be because of verse 4:8, which is a "re-filling" passage. Though he disagrees with Ervin, he does not appear to prove Ervin's view invalid from exegesis. Stronstad's argument is presuppositional.

Stronstad further argues that, based on the context; there is a difference between the function of being filled with the Spirit and full of the Spirit. He argues that "full of the Spirit" describes the Spirit's enabling while "filled with the Spirit" describes prophetic inspiration. This would imply a different meaning in the terms used by Luke to describe the action of the Spirit. Stronstad pioneered the linguistic understanding of the inspiration motif. Stronstad's contribution to this discipline is that Luke used phrases from the prophetic motif to describe the present day outpouring of the Holy Spirit. On this point, Stronstad and Ervin completely agree. In fact, Ervin was arguing the unity of these terms to describe this one event some twenty years prior to Stronstad. But Stronstad diverges from this unity in order to make the term filled categorically different from full. This would be admitting that full is not describing the one event of Pentecost, but some other reality. Though Stronstad pioneered a Lukan theology, he violates his own principles by not connecting the metaphors. This is where Ervin's strength lies. He is consistent in his application of Luke's metaphors.

Stronstad also argues that this event of fullness is a subsequent event, an argument that Ervin aptly defended in his early work.

## Max Turner

Max Turner has become a voice for New Testament scholarship. Turner's book *Power From on High* adds his own insights into Lukan phrases such as filled and full.[229] With extensive exegetical analysis of the terms filled and full, Turner offers an explanation of these terms. Turner argues that the metaphor filled does not indicate fullness in conversion (against the evangelicals), nor confirmation (against the Sacramentalists), nor a state of fullness (against Ervin and Pentecostals).[230] He argues that one is described as filled by "whether the community of Christians *felt the impact of the Spirit* through that person's life and *saw the Spirit's graces and gifts regularly expressed* through him or her."[231] Turner believes that the metaphor is exclusively linked to the Spirit manifesting himself through individuals in speech or power. He gives reference to Ervin's view of the ingressive aorist tense of the verb filled in 2:4 and his view of fullness as a state. He comments, "This forces Ervin to conclude that the aorist at Acts 4:8 refers back to 2:4 while those 'filled with the Spirit' in 4:31 must be other than the 120 of Acts 2:4: i.e. the new converts made from Pentecost onwards."[232] Turner offers no particular critique other than his general premise that Ervin misunderstands the metaphor.

Turner argues that 2:4 does not refer to an inaugural event of fullness. He says, "Acts 2:4 itself thus asserts little more than that within their Pentecost experience the disciples became invasively inspired to speak in tongues."²³³ Turner identifies all of Luke's terms as descriptions of what happened when the Spirit manifested. This is only a metaphor of the work of the Spirit. However, Turner argues that the metaphor "full of" with the genitive, as in the instance of Jesus in Luke 4:1 can "denote a long-term state of affairs, rather than an immediate effect (for which forms of πίμπλημι are preferred.)"²³⁴ Thus for Turner, filled is an action metaphor while *plērēs* is a lasting state. Filled is only a phrase used to describe this momentary action of the Spirit, but full is a state. How does this fit in the greater understanding of the metaphors of the Spirit's immediate activity? By his own reasoning, the state of fullness must be categorically different and thus not truly a Lukan metaphor for prophetic inspiration. This fullness must refer to something completely other than prophetic action. However if Turner did not limit filled to momentary action, then he would agree with Ervin. Ervin believes filled is an act and full is a description of those who had experienced that act of the Spirit.

Turner does not dispute the interpretation of the ingressive aorist; rather he disputes the meaning of the metaphor. He says, "One of the underlying assumptions here is that being 'filled with the Holy Spirit' linguistically connotes the inauguration of some *continuous state* of messianic fullness of the Spirit. But as we have seen earlier, that is to miss the import of the more general metaphor 'to be filled with (some quality)' and to misunderstand the more specific form where 'to be filled with the Spirit' is combined with a verb denoting speech."²³⁵ Essentially for Turner, he argues that Ervin misunderstands the presupposition of the metaphor, not the exegesis. He says, "Luke tends to use the aorist indicative or participle of πίμπλημι + genitive of divine Spirit for events or inspirations of short duration."[236] Being filled only involves immediate inspiration and has no lasting effect. He says, "there is no suggestion that some more enduring endowment is semantically entailed, any more than to say that the people Luke described as 'filled with' 'anger,' 'fear,' 'amazement,' etc., entered a long-term 'state of fullness' of these things."[237] This aorist tense is given as Luke's way of determining short-term empowerment.

But Turner also admits that, "This is not to say that all such aorists necessarily denote short-term punctiliar events; in fact none of the Septuagintal instances with respect to the Spirit pertain to short-term endowments."[238] This is an interesting insight. How can Turner contend that these aorists are only short-term if not all aorist denote short-term events? What makes it short-term? Turner's whole thesis is that Luke borrows terms from the Septuagint in order to give meaning to Luke's account in the Old Testament prophetic understanding. If there are no instances of the aorist pertaining to short-term endowments in the Septuagint, then how can he be sure that this is Luke's intention for Acts 2:4, 4:8, and 4:31? Is the principle that aorists describe a short-term event from the grammar itself or is this a presupposition brought to the text? Turner does not dispute the ingressive aorist as a state of fullness, nor does he prove that all fillings are short-term and not stative. After almost 40 years of new scholarship in the area of pneumatology, it appears to this author that Ervin's view exegetically holds up even in modern scholarship.

## James B. Shelton

James Shelton, New Testament scholar and colleague of Ervin, takes a similar approach to Max Turner. Shelton believes that uses of the term filled are linked to that moment when someone is inspired to speak. He says, "The phrase, 'filled with' or 'full of the Holy Spirit,' indicate primarily that inspired witness about Jesus or against the devil is occurring. Any other significance of the expression is probably peripheral to Luke's intention."[239] For Shelton, the term filled only indicates that what they are saying is inspired. In the instance of Acts 4:8, Shelton argues against Ervin particularly. He says, "Luke describes Peter as filled with the Holy Spirit because at that moment (*plestheis*, aorist participle) Peter was empowered to speak, not because the reader needs a reminder that he had already been filled at Pentecost."[240] He also argues that "Likewise, attempts to identify 4:31ff. as the initial reception of the Spirit for the converts who joined the church as a result of Peter's first sermon comes to ruin under the weight of the immediate context."[241] Shelton does not argue specifically how Ervin's views "come to ruin." He does argue that Peter and John were present at the prayer of 4:24. His argument comes from reason rather than exegesis. His general assumption is that they spoke with boldness because Luke used the term filled.

While Shelton does recognize that Luke uses several terms as synonyms, he uses filled and full only with inspired speech. This would make other terms such as "come upon," "fell on," and "receive" have a different meaning than baptism in the Spirit. He says, "It is true that Luke feels free to interchange the various phrases expressing the coming of the Holy Spirit, for we have seen this in his use of the Holy Spirit filling or coming upon someone in relation to inspired speaking. This substitution of one phrase for another, though somewhat stylistic in places, cannot be viewed as merely random variation."[242] Ervin argues all of Luke's phrases are synonyms for the one experience of baptism in the Spirit. Shelton would argue that Luke's phrases are synonyms but filled has a particular meaning indicating inspired speech. He would disagree with Ervin that all uses of filled/full/came upon/fell on are univocal. Both are arguing for the purpose of the "filling" as empowerment for prophetic speech. Shelton argues that filled is only a metaphor for the reason they are speaking. But why does it have to be momentary? The answer again is an assumption about Luke's purpose for using the term. Because Luke is describing inspired speech, then it is momentary and there is no need for it to last past the speech. Ervin argues that the speech is a consequence of the fulfillment of the promise of the Father. The reason one is filled is to witness.

## *Archie Hui*

Archie Hui seeks to discuss the issues and problems caused by the recent emphasis on the technical uses of filled and full in Acts by scholars like Stronstad, Turner, and Shelton. Hui recognizes the problems and inconsistencies in this view. He says, "Given the larger context or co-texts within Luke-Acts, the Spirit's filling of the disciples is the fulfillment of Jesus' promise of the coming of the Spirit, and it could not possibly be short-term only. While the focus of Acts 2.4 might be on the immediate phenomenon of tongues, it leaves open the door that the presence of the Spirit could be long-term rather than short-term."[243]

Hui is seeking to find a unified understanding in Luke of Spirit-fullness. He recognizes that there are inconsistencies in the formulations by Turner and Shelton for technical understandings of these terms that they admit. He analyzes each argument and concludes, "The two terms do not differ in terms of the duration of Spirit-fullness; short-term ('filled with the Holy Spirit') versus long-term ('full of the Holy Spirit'). They primarily address the question of extent (how much a person is influenced by the Spirit; a lot or not at all) and not the question of duration (how long is a person influenced by the Spirit; long or short). They differ in that one ('filled with the Spirit') is inceptive or constative, while the other ('full of the Holy Spirit') is stative."[244] Hui argues that these terms do not indicate how long one is inspired, but how they are inspired. He is reflecting the same concept Ervin argues for. Being filled with the Spirit is the event that initiates the state of fullness that causes the prophetic/inspired speech. Hui is one of the few scholars who have argued against the technical terms.

In the footnotes, Hui identifies Ervin's view in particular as "somewhat unusual."[245] He questions Ervin's view fully because it "raises more questions than it answers."[246] First he questions why Luke uses the term filled for Elizabeth's experience. He asks, "Are they baptized in the Spirit too?" Ervin argues that these fillings were in the Old Testament pattern of prophetic inspiration, since they are before the death and resurrection and during the larger scope of the salvation event. He says, "These examples, while informative are not normative for Christian experience."²⁴⁷ Essentially he argues that the motif is the same (inspiration), but the nature of the event is different from a covenantal standpoint.

Hui's second question is "If Ervin is right to think that such baptism in the Spirit leads all Christians into the Spirit-filled state, then why did Luke note that only some Christians are 'full of the Spirit?"²⁴⁸ This question is misleading. Though Ervin believes that all Christians can be filled with the Spirit, not all Christians are filled with the Spirit. Ervin says, "Men already 'full' of the Spirit were chosen to fill this office. Stephen had been filled with the Spirit of God on a prior occasion."²⁴⁹ Ervin in no way argues that all people are filled with the Spirit. Some are not, but can be. This is the case in 4:31. Some of the converts made between 2:4 and 4:31 had not yet been filled until the prayer for boldness. These "problems" are not problems at all. A comprehensive understanding of Ervin's pneumatology answers all the questions that rise from scholars' reading of his works. Yet, these questions do not substantiate any significant rebuttal of his views. Most of the issues are peripheral, yet Ervin does provide in his works the answers to all of the critics' questions.

## *Larry D. Hart*

Charismatic scholar and colleague of Ervin, Larry Hart, tries to offer a solution to the discussion between Pentecostals and evangelicals about the nature of Spirit baptism. He offers a solution that declares "both are right."²⁵⁰ Larry Hart offers a broader definition that would include both Luke and Paul. He says, "In the Pauline sense of the metaphor, all believers have experienced Spirit baptism. In the Lukan emphasis on the empowering dimension of the Spirit baptism, we may not all be 'filled with the Spirit.'"[251] He expands the metaphor of Spirit baptism to include salvation and empowerment. This is a helpful contribution because it helps give both Pentecostals and evangelicals common ground to discuss this issue.

As a student and eventual colleague of Ervin, Larry Hart understands that Luke is using synonyms such as baptized, come upon, filled, poured out, etc. Hart recognizes that Luke "uses seven different phrases to describe the coming of the Spirit."[252] But he rejects the traditional Pentecostal view of subsequence. He says, "Thus, when Peter referred, in his Pentecost sermon, to receiving the 'promise of the Father;' and the 'gift of the Holy Spirit' . . . he was referring to both conversion and charisma! Whenever people 'received the Holy Spirit' or 'received the gift of the Holy Spirit' or were 'baptized in the Holy Spirit' in Acts that is, whenever they became Christians the Charismatic dimension was already present in their lives!"[253] Hart is not opposed to the empowerment metaphor, but he also includes the salvation aspect. In this he represents many Charismatic traditions that believe that the Spirit is present in us at salvation but needs to be released in the charismatic dimension. Can Hart argue that Luke does mean salvation in his metaphor of baptism in the Spirit? Though an integrated theology of Paul and Luke can mean that Spirit baptism can mean salvation and empowerment, Ervin would argue that this is not what Luke specifically means in Acts. If Spirit baptism or filling refers to "becoming Christians" then why does he find "another filling" in the Acts narrative?²⁵⁴ Though his integrative approach is helpful for a New Testament understanding of the term baptism in the Spirit, Hart insists that Luke's terms are communicating salvation and empowerment. Paul may be able to communicate this idea, but Ervin would argue Luke does not.

Dr. Hart integrates into his theology Paul's view of "filled" from Ephesians 5:18 in order to talk about a fullness that can be maintained. He uses this text to show that both Pentecostals and evangelicals should admit that whatever baptism in the Spirit is, the believer needs to have continual fullness. This point is well made. The question is why is re-filling necessary? The imperative to be continuously filled, even if Lukan in origin, does not reflect the need for "future fillings."²⁵⁵ It argues for a continual state of fullness. Ervin argues that continuous filling is consistent with the Lukan understanding of the state of being filled with the Spirit. He argues that a view of repeated filling is not the message of this passage. Ervin says, "Since the continuous (durative) idea is grammatically and contextually preferable to the iterative (repeated) sense of the verb 'be filled,' it follows that this passage does not teach repeated fillings with the Holy Spirit."²⁵⁶ Ervin's argument does show that this verse does not say "be filled over and over." It does encourage people to be filled with a continual fullness. It is this continual nature of "being filled" that pushes Ervin's critics from the idea of one filling. Integration with Paul is important for a full understanding of the New Testament. Ervin argues that one enters a state of continual fullness. However, "be baptized over and over in the Spirit" would not be a helpful understanding for Charismatics or evangelicals. This is the danger of integrating Luke and Paul.

## *Frank D. Macchia*

Modern Pentecostal scholar Frank D. Macchia proposes a modern, global understanding of Spirit baptism. In his work, *Baptized in the Spirit: A Global Pentecostal Theology*, Macchia claims, "Not since Harold Hunter's and Howard Ervin's treatments of the doctrine published nearly two decades ago has there been a similar effort to write a theology of Spirit baptism."[257] Macchia builds on all of the advancements of previous Lukan scholars in hopes of building a global Pentecostal theology. He suggests that the metaphor of Spirit baptism must be expanded to include not only empowerment, but salvation and sanctification as well. This expansion provides a way forward in the debate toward reconciliation. He says, "The older tendency was to see Spirit baptism as a separate reception of the Spirit that functioned as a rite of passage to spiritual fullness and spiritual gifts. What I regard to be a more helpful trend, the tendency now among many Pentecostals is to accent the gift of the Spirit given in regeneration and to view the Pentecostal experience of Spirit baptism as empowerment for witness as a 'release' of an already-indwelling Spirit in life."[258]

 This reflects the general attitude of many Charismatic scholars with regard to the nature of the Spirit's relation between his work in salvation and the empowerment of the Spirit. This is the same concept that Larry Hart advocates. The question that arises with this view is a question of the nature of the metaphors. With statements in Luke such as fell upon/came on/poured out/comes upon, how would these metaphors be helpful for understanding a release of the Spirit that already exists? In his quest for a global Pentecostal theology, Macchia maintains the Pentecostal understanding of empowerment and builds on the theology of Stronstad, Anthony Palma, and others. Macchia does mention Ervin on several occasions concerning the development of his own Pentecostal theology.

## OTHER SCHOLARS RESPOND

Some other scholars who did not interact with Ervin specifically made comments about the issue of refilling. Evangelical scholar Andreas J. Kostenberger asks the question about what it means to be filled. His article deals primarily with whether a believer needs to ask to be filled with the Spirit. But in an interesting comment about Acts 4, he says, "In 4:8 Peter, 'after having been filled with the Holy Spirit,' gives his defense to the Sanhedrin for his healing of the lame man. In Acts 4:31, immediately following this defense the believers, when they had prayed but not necessarily asked to be filled with the Holy Spirit, were filled with the Spirit with the result that they spoke the word of God with boldness."[259] Kostenberger does not indicate when Peter was filled, but does reflect the alternate understanding of Acts 4:8. The question of when this filling occurred could be reasonably assumed to have happened in Acts 2:4. This is Ervin's argument. There is nothing to mandate that Peter's filling had to be immediate. He finishes his article commenting, "The difference between the references to being 'filled with' and being 'full of' the Spirit appears to be essentially one of event versus general characteristic."[260] Kostenberger recognizes that filled is initiatory and full is a characteristic. This would be consistent with Ervin.

New Testament scholar Ben Witherington admits that "These terms can be and are used by Luke interchangeably, and cannot be treated as technical terms or be neatly parceled out to line up a chronology of different spiritual experiences."[261] Witherington recognizes that Luke does not use these terms to describe different events. He knows that all terms are synonyms for the same event. Witherington reflects the common view of repeated fillings by viewing Acts 4:8 and 4:31 as additional fillings. He brings this belief into his exegesis. He says, "The verb 'filled' (*eplesthesan*) in v. 4 is an important one. Elsewhere in Luke-Acts it describes an initial endowment of someone by the Spirit for service, or when they are inspired to speak God's word (Acts 4:8, 31; 13:9). . . . Related forms of this verb can be used to describe repeated fillings or the continuous filling of the Christian (Acts 13:52; Eph.5:18)."[262] Witherington recognizes the terms are synonymous but makes Acts 13:52 and Ephesians 5:18 exceptions to this rule. He also admits that 4:8 and 4:31 are terms that describe "initial." If they are describing the initial giving of the Spirit, then Peter would be initially empowered in 4:8 and re-initially empowered in 4:31. It is unclear what Dr. Witherington means by these statements. There is no clear explanation of what is happening in 4:8 and 4:31.

Craig Keener likewise recognizes the nature of Luke's phrases. He says that Luke "uses a variety of synonymous expressions that it identifies with one another and that it applies theses experiences of empowerment."²⁶³ While he recognized the synonymous expressions, he says that these empowerments can happen over and over. He says, "Acts indicates that believers may receive empowerments subsequent to their 'second experience' (4:8, 31; 13:9)."²⁶⁴ His point is that everyone argues for more than one experience with the Holy Spirit. However, in doing so, he admits that all fillings are not sufficient. He does not deal with Ervin, but reflects the same presupposition as the former scholars.

French L. Arrington takes a unique spin on the refilling passage. He claims, "The context of each indicates that *pimplemi* is used when there was a deficiency in the lives of believers. . . . The use of *pimplemi* implies spiritual deficiency."²⁶⁵ This would have to be proven from Scripture. We have no evidence that there was ever any deficiency in Peter that would make him need an additional filling. Peter was not only filled in 2:4, but in 4:8 he is declared as filled just 20 verses prior to another so-called filling. The burden lies on the scholar to provide some sort of deficiency in those 20 verses. It is doubtful that this is Luke's intent. He concludes that "as well as the initial infilling with the Spirit there are fillings for a specific need or task."²⁶⁶ What is present in his statement is the assumption that special fillings are needed that previous fillings could not fulfill. This is the deficiency that necessitates a refilling. This view seems to be pure speculation that is not supported by any evidence of Peter's deficiency.

Eduard Schweizer believes that the gift of the Spirit is the conversion experience. He says, "Thus we read in Acts 5:32 that God has given the Holy Spirit to those who obey him. That is not something that happens merely on a single occasion. Although the Spirit conditions the whole of a person's life, yet on specific occasions he is given anew."[267] Evangelicals insist that one is baptized in the Spirit (salvation) once but he must be given anew at times. Schweizer reflects the same assumption that filled and baptized are two different works.

Sacramentalists do not have a good answer for these passages either. Noted Charismatic-Catholic scholar and Dialogue partner of Ervin, Fr. Killian McDonnell, addresses 4:31. He says, "It portrays a second coming of the Holy Spirit, not immediately in a sacramental context but in answer to prayer."[268] For Sacramentalists, baptism in the Spirit comes in the form of baptism into the Church. This passage would be describing a second work in their theology. Sacramentalists would need to make this passage a second baptism in the Spirit to have a subsequent filling. This is exactly what Fr. McDonnell does when he says, "This is important data to incorporate into our conclusion about the modern phenomenon of the later coming of the Holy Spirit upon Christians already baptized."[269] McDonnell is not addressing re-filling, but he is allowing for additional givings of the Spirit to substantiate the charismatic renewal.

**CONCLUSION**

From the early days of Ervin's writings, both evangelical and Pentecostal scholars have taken occasion to respond to his views. The ongoing critique of Ervin's theology and exegesis has held up under the scrutiny of some of the Church's best scholars yet few have been able to diminish his arguments for "One Baptism-One Filling." The strength of Howard Ervin's view of Spirit baptism is that he remains consistent. He argues that Luke describes the baptism in the Spirit as being filled with the Spirit. He also argues that when Peter is filled with the Spirit in Acts 4:8 that Luke is referring to Peter's previous filling as an adjective (the Spirit-filled Peter). He also argues that Acts 4:31 does not reflect a fresh filling; rather he is describing the filling of the believers that are with Peter so that they are all empowered to speak the word boldly. This view keeps Luke's terms consistent. One must either make filling something other than baptism and misunderstand Luke, or make similar terms mean different things, such as filled and full. This inconsistency appears to be confusing and unnecessary. If the filling in 2:4 is a state entered into, then all other phrases can be explained. Dr. Ervin's views are as sound today as they were when he wrote them. He continues to show his commitment to the text and provides quality scholarship to the Pentecostal community.

## Chapter Six

# A Call for Re-Examination

Howard M. Ervin's "Pilgrimage into Pentecost" has left a pneumatological legacy that should be cherished today and be cultivated in the next generation. Ervin's influence reaches from the university to the local church. He is respected by Pentecostals, Evangelicals, and Sacramentalists. His work with Full Gospel Business Men's Fellowship International brought the message of Pentecost to people from all backgrounds who desired to experience the reality of the Holy Spirit in their life. His scholarly works are recognized by early Pentecostals as groundbreaking exegetical defenses of Pentecostalism. His influence on the students and faculty of Oral Roberts University has spanned 40 years. These students have brought the message of Pentecost all around the world. Ervin's ministry in the years of Oral Roberts Partners Seminars impacted thousands. He was able to lead thousands into the baptism in the Holy Spirit in these meetings. Howard Ervin's presence has truly been felt by people around the world.

Ervin's life was a journey into Pentecostal scholarship. Howard Ervin was at the cutting edge of Pentecostal apologetics when he produced his first book, *These Are Not Drunken, As Ye Suppose,* in 1968. Ervin was arguing exegetically before many other Pentecostal scholars were. Ervin wrote in a time when many Pentecostals focused on the practical and experiential and were not necessarily interested in the exegesis of Pentecost. Ervin helped pave the way for the explosion of work in the area of pneumatology and Luke-Acts in particular. In this way, his books may have come before their time.

Howard Ervin helped open the door for Pentecost to reach the highest levels of the academic world. His legacy is one of strong commitment to the text. As Pentecostal scholars continue to advance the discipline of understanding the unique Lukan theology of the Spirit, Ervin reminds us to stay faithful to the text. Many have moved on past Ervin's theology and exegesis. While there is great admiration by the generation that stood on his shoulders, the next generation may not recognize the groundbreaking work of men like Ervin. As the Society for Pentecostal Studies continues to give Pentecostal scholars the opportunity to advance the work of Pentecostal theology, there can be a tendency to advance Pentecostal theology for advancement's sake. Many today are exploring the subtle nuances of Lukan terminology and from it crafting new understandings of Pentecostal belief. While the arena of biblical studies is by no means exhausted, Pentecostal scholars must resist the urge to turn true biblical investigation into a quest for novelty.

Scholars need to stand on the shoulders of men like Ervin and not dismiss their work because it is old. Ervin's insights into the theology of Pentecost are foundations to be built upon. Many scholars today find Ervin to be irrelevant to today's discussion. People question whether his approach to theology is too ridged and outdated, but his theology is a theology that tries to take the context seriously. Ervin endeavored to remain faithful to the immediate context and resisted the urge to look to the text to prove a theological presupposition. In a culture that loves to dismiss the past and relishes novelty, Pentecostals must be very careful that our scholarship does not cause Pentecostalism to drift from its solid foundation on good exegesis.

There are important lessons to be learned from Howard Ervin's pilgrimage into Pentecost. First, Pentecostals can be the best of scholars. Ervin has the best education and highest degrees that a scholar can have. His education became the vehicle for him embracing the Pentecostal message. The Pentecostal message is one that is grounded in good exegesis and sound theology. Pentecostals never have to be ashamed of their theology. It has been tested in the arena of academic debate and has held up under the scrutiny of some of the finest minds. Whereas past generations have been suspicions of academic pursuits, Ervin's legacy demonstrates the fact that scholarship can be an ally in the mission of proclaiming the Pentecostal message. The next generation of Pentecostals can fully embrace academia as a medium for Pentecostal apologetics. Ervin was committed to the text. He was convinced by the Scriptures that Pentecost was true. Ervin's legacy is one that can inspire future Pentecostal scholarship to continue to advance a Pentecostal faith that is grounded in the Word of God.

Secondly, Howard Ervin's pilgrimage into Pentecost inspired an emphasis on unity within the body of Christ. He truly believed that the Holy Spirit could inspire the unity that Christ desires for his Church. As people of all expressions of faith share the experience of a vibrant relationship with God through the Holy Spirit, walls of division will come down and true *koinonia* can be achieved. Ervin's life began in bigotry, but was transformed into true ecumenism. The next generation of Pentecostals are hungry for authentic Christian unity. Many have been turned away from or left Pentecostalism because of a perceived sectarian philosophy inherent in Pentecost. Some have argued that what makes the Pentecostal message distinct is also what has kept people from Pentecost. Because of this, some have changed their message in order to reach out to a broader audience.

Howard Ervin is an example of how Pentecost can translate to people of all communions of Christianity without changing the message. He is convinced that Pentecost is grounded in good theology and sound exegesis. Ervin can be very persuasive in defending Pentecost apologetically. But, rather than trying to persuade people to his theology, Ervin simply offered the invitation to an experience. His books contain his theology, but the message he preached was primarily his testimony. He did not waste time arguing against people's theology when he preached. He would simply lead them to the Scriptures and tell of how the apostle's experience had been repeated in his own life.

When a believer is baptized in the Spirit, they have a common experience that transcends theology and builds bridges into true communion. Our dogmas may divide us theologically, but the Holy Spirit can unite the Church. Unity is more than uniformity. Uniformity tries to make others look like them. Unity looks past the differences and finds the commonality shared by those who are different. Ervin did not try to make all believers into Pentecostals. He believed that believers should remain in their own traditions but find commonality in their experiences with the Spirit. Sectarianism is born out of an attempt to codify dogma that distinguishes one from another. Unity is born when people all share the same experience and share in communion based on that experience. When we know that we share the same Spirit, we can discuss our differences without insecurity. Theological debate can polarize if not shared in communion. Pentecost allows the Spirit of Truth to open our lives to inspection of our beliefs and begins a dialogue with the Spirit in others.

Perhaps Ervin's greatest contribution was in the lives of the people that he ministered to. His congregation benefited from his honest investigation of the Word of God. Many of them followed Ervin as he ministered all over the world. Emmanuel Baptist Church learned how to be a global community of faith. Ervin served the Baptist tradition by leading the Charismatic Baptist movement and building up his fellow Baptist ministers. Believers from mainline Protestant denominations found a voice for an authentic relationship with God and true experience with the Spirit that was responsible and dignified. Many of Dr. Ervin's colleagues on the faculty of Oral Roberts University find him to be the standard of excellence and scholarship that should be emulated in their own lives. Many of the faculty were once his students and carry on his legacy in their own teaching and scholarship. He leaves a legacy of commitment to excellence and Spirit-empowered ministry. His students have been impacted by his scholarly commitment to education and his teaching on the Spirit-filled life. Howard Ervin's legacy is the impact his life and ministry had on individuals. This author was greatly impacted by Dr. Ervin's commitment to scholarship with a pastor's heart. His pneumatology class showed this author that one can be both Pentecostal and sound in one's theology and exegesis. Ervin exemplifies the commitment to the Word and Spirit.

This work is a call for Pentecostals to once again re-examine his teaching on Spirit-baptism and discover the strength of his theology for Pentecostals. Ervin will not be accepted by everyone, but Pentecostals can take advantage of the commitment to Scripture and the quality of scholarship that Ervin brings to the debate. Though his works were written in a different time, the message is still valid for today. The pneumatological legacy of Dr. Howard M. Ervin can live on in the next generation of Pentecostals who rediscover the strength of his message and continue to proclaim it as we work to reach the world for Jesus Christ.

# About the Author

Daniel D. Isgrigg became a licensed minister with the Assemblies of God in 2004 and became ordained in 2006. In 1997, Daniel entered Oral Roberts University and studied theology and church history. He received the Bachelor of Arts in 2000, for which his thesis treated the theology of Irenaeus. Daniel earned the Master of Arts in Theological and Historical Studies in May, 2007, also from Oral Roberts University. His M.A. thesis on Howard M. Ervin's Pentecostal theology is the basis for the present study. Currently Daniel is the Associate Pastor at Christian Chapel, an Assemblies of God church in Tulsa, Oklahoma. He has served on the pastoral staff since 1998 in the area of Christian Education. Daniel is a member of the Society of Pentecostal Studies. He has also written a book on eschatology titled *Why I Want to Be Left Behind*, also published by Word & Spirit Press (ISBN 0-9785352-5-1). He is married to Amonda Matthewman Isgrigg, and they are expecting their first child.

# Notes

1. Howard M. Ervin, Professor of Old Testament at Oral Roberts University, interview by author, Tulsa, OK, 8 January 2008.

2. Howard M. Ervin, "Pilgrimage into Pentecost," Ervin Publications, Holy Spirit Research Center, Oral Roberts University, Tulsa, OK, n.d., audiocassette.

3. Howard M. Ervin, "Testimony" Day of Renewal at St. Nicholas Catholic Charismatic Center, Oct 1978. Holy Spirit Research Center, Oral Roberts University, Tulsa, OK. Audio cassette recording. Ervin commented that his congregation was not only difficult but they were unimpressed with his credentials and speech.

4. Howard M. Ervin, Professor of Old Testament at Oral Roberts University, interview by author, Tulsa, OK, 9 February 2006.

5. Ervin, interview by author, 9 February 2006.

6. Ervin, interview by author, 9 February 2006.

7. P. H. Alexander, "Ervin, Howard Matthew," *Dictionary of Pentecostal and Charismatic Movements,* ed. Stanley Burgess and Gary B. McGee (Grand Rapids: Zondervan, 1988), 263.

8. Ervin, "Testimony," Oct 1978.

9. The only written information about Ervin's tenure at Central Baptist Church is contained in "One Hundredth Anniversary 1893–1993" booklet produced by Central Baptist Church, Atlantic Highlands, New Jersey, 1993. The controversy and circumstances that let to Ervin's resignation and the founding of Emmanuel Baptist Church are documented in this booklet.

10. Charles Farrah and Steve Durasoff, "Biographical and Bibliographical Sketch," in *Essays on Apostolic Themes: Studies in Honor of Howard M. Ervin Presented to Him by Colleagues and Friends on his Sixty-Fifth Birthday,* ed. Paul Elbert (Peabody, MA: Hendrickson, 1985), xi.

11. Howard M. Ervin, *These Are Not Drunken, As Ye Suppose.* (Plainfield, NJ: Logos Publishing, 1968). Dedication.

12. Elizabeth Porter, "Dr. Howard Ervin Retires after 40 Years of Teaching." *The University Oracle,* 8 December 2006, sec. A, p. 2.

13. Ervin, "Pilgrimage into Pentecost."

14. Ervin, "Pilgrimage into Pentecost."
15. Ervin, "Pilgrimage into Pentecost."
16. Ervin, "Pilgrimage into Pentecost."
17. Ervin, "Pilgrimage into Pentecost."
18. Ervin, "Pilgrimage into Pentecost."
19. Ervin, "Pilgrimage into Pentecost."
20. Ervin, "Pilgrimage into Pentecost."
21. Ervin, "Pilgrimage into Pentecost."
22. Howard M. Ervin, "My Testimony," Holy Spirit Research Center, Oral Roberts University, Tulsa, OK, 1968, audiocassette.
23. McCandlish Phillips, "And There Appeared To Them Tongues Of Fire." *Saturday Evening Post*, 16, May, 1964, 31.
24. Howard M. Ervin, "A Rationale for Tongues," First American Baptist Conference on the Holy Spirit, Holy Spirit Research Center, Oral Roberts University, 10 September 1975, audiocassette.
25. Howard M. Ervin, "My Testimony," Holy Spirit Research Center, Oral Roberts University, Tulsa, OK, 3 October 1969, audiocassette.
26. Phillips, 31.
27. Paul Elbert, "Editors Preface," in *Essays on Apostolic Themes: Studies in Honor of Howard M. Ervin Presented to Him by Colleagues and Friends on his Sixty-Fifth Birthday.* ed. Paul Elbert (Peabody, MA: Hendrickson, 1985), xii.
28. Ervin, "Pilgrimage into Pentecost."
29. David Edwin Harrell, Jr. *Oral Roberts: An American Life* (Bloomington, IN: Indiana University Press, 1985), 216.
30. A biography of Oral Roberts by David Edwin Harrell Jr. records, "The list of speakers included Baptist pastor Howard M. Ervin, a rising leader in the charismatic movement." Harrell, 216.
31. Howard M. Ervin, "For Such a Time as This." *Outreach*, no. 1 (1965): 24.
32. Howard M. Ervin, Professor of Old Testament at Oral Roberts University, interview by author, Tulsa, OK, 26 February 2007.
33. Letter to Howard Ervin read by Dr. Ralph Fagin, Vice President for Academic Affairs, "Howard M. Ervin Retirement Reception," Oral Roberts University, Tulsa, OK, 5 December 2006, Mp3 recording by author.
34. Farrah and Durasoff, xii.

35. Elizabeth Porter, "Dr. Howard Ervin Retires after 40 Years of Teaching." *The University Oracle,* 8 December 2006, sec. A, p. 2.

36. Thomson K. Mathew, Dean of School of Theology and Missions, "Howard M. Ervin Retirement Reception," Oral Roberts University, 5 December 2006, Mp3 recording by author.

37. Ervin, "Pilgrimage into Pentecost."

38. Farrah and Durasoff, xii.

39. Ervin, *Conversion-Initiation and Baptism in the Holy Spirit.* (Peabody, MA: Hendrickson, 1984). v, viii. He often discusses the anti-sacramental presuppositions of James Dunn. Ervin argues that baptismal regeneration argues for subsequent Spirit baptism against the conversion-initiation paradigm.

40. Howard Ervin, "Testimony" Day of Renewal at St. Nicholas Catholic Charismatic Center, Holy Spirit Research Center, Oral Roberts University, Tulsa, OK. October 1978. Audio cassette recording.

41. Ervin, "Testimony." October 1978.

42. Killian McDonnell, "Improbable Conversation: The International Classical Pentecostal/Roman Catholic Dialogue" *Pneuma* no 2, Fall 1995.

43. Ervin, "My Testimony," 1968, Audio cassette recording.

44. Ervin, "My Testimony," 1968, Audio cassette recording.

45. Howard M. Ervin, "Refilled" Lecture from GTHE 692 Pneumatology, Oral Roberts University. 2 February 2006. Mp3 recording by author.

46. Ervin, "Refilled." 2 February 2006.

47. Howard M. Ervin, *This Which Ye See and Hear* (Plainfield, NJ: Logos, 1972), 59.

48. Howard M. Ervin, "A Rationale for Tongues," First American Baptist Conference on the Holy Spirit, Holy Spirit Research Center, Oral Roberts University, 10 September 1975, audiocassette.

49. Gary Clarke, Chairman of Holy Spirit Renewal Ministries in American Baptist Churches, interview by author, Cleveland, TN, 9 March 2007.

50. Thomson K. Mathew, Dean of School of Theology and Missions, "Howard M. Ervin Retirement Reception," Oral Roberts University, 5 December 2006, Mp3 recording by author.

51. Mathew, 5 December 2006.

52. Lederle, 95.

53. Menzies, William (wwmnezies@mchsi.com), Reply to Query Regarding Howard M. Ervin. e-mail to Daniel D. Isgrigg (danny@christianchapel.com) (7 January 2007).

54. Ervin, *These Are Not Drunken, As Ye Suppose* (Plainfield, NJ: Logos Publishing, 1968).

55. Paul Elbert, interview by author, Cleveland, TN, 10 February, 2007.

56. Paul Elbert, "Author's Preface." *Essays on Apostolic Themes: Studies in Honor of Howard M. Ervin Presented to him by Colleagues and friends on his Sixty-Fifth Birthday,* ed. Paul Elbert (Peabody, MA: Hendrickson, 1985), v.

57. Paul Elbert, 10 February, 2007.

58. James Forbes, "Foreword," in *Essays on Apostolic Themes: Studies in Honor of Howard M. Ervin Presented to him by Colleagues and friends on his Sixty-Fifth Birthday,* ed. Paul Elbert (Peabody, MA: Hendrickson, 1985), xix.

59. James D. G. Dunn, "Romans 7:14–25 in the Theology of Paul," *Essays on Apostolic Themes: Studies in Honor of Howard M. Ervin Presented to Him by Colleagues and Friends on His Sixty-Fifth Birthday,* ed. Paul Elbert (Peabody, MA: Hendrickson, 1985), 49.

60. Robert Graves (rgraves@tffps.org), Reply to Query Regarding Howard M. Ervin, e-mail to Daniel D. Isgrigg (danny@christianchapel.com) (3 January 2007).

61. Graves, 3 January 2007.

62. James D. G. Dunn *Baptism in the Holy Spirit* (London: SCM Press, 1970).

63. Dunn *Baptism in the Holy Spirit*, 231.

64. Dunn, *Baptism in the Holy Spirit*, 70.

65. Dunn, *Baptism in the Holy Spirit*, 128.

66. Dunn, *Baptism in the Holy Spirit*, 171.

67. Dunn, *Baptism in the Holy Spirit*, 23.

68. Howard M. Ervin, interview by Robert W. Graves, President of the Foundation for Pentecostal Scholarship, Tulsa OK, November 1980, audiocassette.

69. Ervin, interview by Robert Graves, November 1980.

70. Ervin, interview by Robert Graves, November 1980.

71. Ervin, *Conversion-Initiation and Baptism in the Holy Spirit*, vi.

72. Ervin, interview by author, 26 February 2007.
73. Ervin, *Conversion-Initiation and Baptism in the Holy Spirit*, vi.
74. Ervin, *Conversion-Initiation and Baptism in the Holy Spirit*, 35.
75. Ervin, *These Are Not Drunken, As Ye Suppose*.
76. Howard M. Ervin, *And Forbid Not To Speak With Tongues* (Plainfield, NJ: Logos Publishing, 1971).
77. Howard M. Ervin, *That Which You See and Hear* (Plainfield, NJ: Logos Publishing, 1972).
78. *The Layman's Commentary on the Holy Spirit*, ed. John Rae (Plainfield, NJ: Logos International, 1972)
79. Ervin, *Conversion-Initiation and Baptism in the Holy Spirit*.
80. Howard M. Ervin, *Spirit Baptism: A Biblical Investigation* (Peabody, MA: Hendrickson Publishers, 1987).
81. Howard M. Ervin, *Healing: Sign of the Kingdom* (Peabody, MA: Hendrickson, 2002).
82. Ervin, *Spirit Baptism*, 25.
83. Ervin, *Spirit Baptism*, 25–26.
84. Ervin, *Spirit Baptism*, 25.
85. Ervin, *Spirit Baptism*, 27.
86. Ervin, *Spirit Baptism*, 44.
87. Ervin, *Spirit Baptism*, 25.
88. Ervin, *These Are Not Drunken, As Ye Suppose*, 27.
89. Ervin, *These Are Not Drunken, As Ye Suppose*, 31–31.
90. Ervin, *Conversion-Initiation and Baptism in the Holy Spirit*, 16.
91. Ervin, *Spirit Baptism*, 25.
92. Ervin, *Spirit Baptism*, 24.
93. Ervin, *Spirit Baptism*, 25.
94. Ervin, *Spirit Baptism*, 24.
95. Ervin, *Spirit Baptism*, 24.
96. Ervin, *Spirit Baptism*, 33.
97. Ervin, *These Are Not Drunken, As Ye Suppose*, 51.
98. Ervin, *These Are Not Drunken, As Ye Suppose*, 52.

99. Ervin, *These Are Not Drunken, As Ye Suppose*, 53.

100. Howard M. Ervin, *That Which Ye See and Hear* (Plainfield, NJ: Logos, 1973), 29.

101. Ervin, *That Which Ye See and Hear* (Plainfield, NJ: Logos, 1973), 26–27

102. Ervin, *Spirit Baptism*, 104.

103. Ervin, *Spirit Baptism*, 103.

104. See Ervin, *That Which Ye See and Hear*, 26–27. also, Ervin, *These Are Not Drunken, As Ye Suppose*, 51–53.

105. Ervin, *That Which Ye See and Hear*, 25–26

106. Ervin, *That Which Ye See and Hear*, 30.

107. Ervin, *Spirit Baptism*, 81.

108. Russell Rathbun, *Post Rapture Radio* (San Francisco: Jossey-Bass, 1995), 141.

109. Rathbun, 145.

110. Ervin, *Spirit Baptism*, 42.

111. Ervin, *Spirit Baptism*, 43.

112. Ervin, *Conversion-Initiation and Baptism in the Holy Spirit*, 5.

113. Ervin, *Conversion-Initiation and Baptism in the Holy Spirit*, 6.

114. Ervin, *Spirit Baptism*, 38.

115. Ervin, *Spirit Baptism*, 70.

116. Ervin, *Spirit Baptism*, 72.

117. Ervin, *Spirit Baptism*, 73.

118. Ervin, *Spirit Baptism*, 74.

119. See Ervin, *Conversion-Initiation and Baptism in the Holy Spirit*, 41–44.

120. Ervin, *Spirit Baptism*, 76.

121. Ervin, *Spirit Baptism*, 77.

122. Ervin, *Spirit Baptism*, 78.

123. Ervin, *Conversion-Initiation and Baptism in the Holy Spirit*, 52.

124. Ervin, *Conversion-Initiation and Baptism in the Holy Spirit*, 58ff.

125. Ervin, *Spirit Baptism*, 80.

— Notes

126. Ervin, *Spirit Baptism*, 84.
127. Ervin, *Spirit Baptism*, 88.
128. Ervin, *Spirit Baptism*, 92.
129. Ervin, *Spirit Baptism*, 92.
130. Ervin, *Spirit Baptism*, 84.
131. Ervin, *Spirit Baptism*, 109.
132. This subject is covered at length in his book *Healing: Sign of the Kingdom* (2002).
133. Ervin, *Healing: Sign of the Kingdom*, 12.
134. Ervin, *Healing: Sign of the Kingdom*, 12.
135. See Ervin, *Healing: Sign of the Kingdom*, 14–23.
136. Ervin, interview with Robert Graves, November 1980.
137. Ervin, interview by author, 26 February 2007.
138. Ervin, interview by author, 26 February 2007.
139. Ervin, interview by author, 26 February 2007.
140. Ervin, *Spirit Baptism,* 25–26.
141. Ervin, *Spirit Baptism,* 49–50.
142. Ervin, *These Are Not Drunken, As Ye Suppose,* 58.
143. Ervin, *Spirit Baptism,* 45.
144. Ervin, *These Are Not Drunken, As Ye Suppose*, 61.
145. Ervin, *Conversion-Initiation and Baptism in the Holy Spirit*, 39.
146. Ervin, *Spirit Baptism,* 1.
147. Ervin, *Spirit Baptism,* 1.
148. Ervin, *That Which You See and Hear*, 83.
149. Ervin, *That Which You See and Hear*, 83.
150. Howard M. Ervin, "Filled Continuously", Holy Spirit Research Center, Oral Roberts University, Tulsa, OK, 1980, audiocassette.
151. Ervin, "Filled Continuously."
152. Ervin, *That Which You See And Here*, 83.
153. Ervin, *That Which You See And Here*, 84.

154. Ervin, *That Which You See And Here*, 84.

155. Ervin, *That Which You See And Here*, 86.

156. *Perichoresis* is the theological concept of the mutual indwelling and penetrating within the persons of the Trinity.

157. Ervin, *Spirit Baptism*, 45.

158. Ervin, *Spirit Baptism*, 45.

159. Ervin, *These Are Not Drunken, As Ye Suppose*, 59.

160. Ervin, *These Are Not Drunken, As Ye Suppose*, 59.

161. Ervin, *These Are Not Drunken, As Ye Suppose*, 67.

162. Ervin, *These Are Not Drunken, As Ye Suppose*, 67.

163. Ervin, *These Are Not Drunken, As Ye Suppose*, 67.

164. Ervin, *Spirit Baptism*, 46.

165. Ervin, *Conversion-Initiation and Baptism in the Holy Spirit*, 36.

166. Ervin, *Spirit Baptism*, 47.

167. Ervin, *Spirit Baptism*, 47.

168. Ervin, *Conversion-Initiation and Baptism in the Holy Spirit*, 39.

169. Ervin, *Conversion-Initiation*, 39.

170. Ervin, *Conversion-Initiation*, 39.

171. Ervin, *Spirit Baptism*, 46.

172. James Dunn, *Baptism in the Holy Spirit* (London: SCM Press, 1970), 70.

173. Ervin, *Spirit Baptism*, 69.

174. Howard M. Ervin, "John's Pneumatology," lecture from GTHE 692 Pneumatology, Oral Roberts University, Tulsa, OK, 2 February 2006, Mp3 recording by author.

175. Ervin, *These Are Not Drunken, As Ye Suppose*, 65.

176. Ervin, *These Are Not Drunken, As Ye Suppose*, 65.

177. Ervin, *These Are Not Drunken, As Ye Suppose*, 67.

178. Ervin, *Conversion-Initiation and Baptism in the Holy Spirit*, 38.

179. Ervin, *Conversion-Initiation and Baptism in the Holy Spirit*, 38.

180. Ervin, *Conversion-Initiation and Baptism in the Holy Spirit*, 38.

Notes

181. Ervin, *Conversion-Initiation and Baptism in the Holy Spirit*, 36.
182. Ervin, *Conversion-Initiation and Baptism in the Holy Spirit*, vii.
183. Ervin, *Conversion-Initiation and Baptism in the Holy Spirit*, 11.
184. Ervin, *Conversion-Initiation and Baptism in the Holy Spirit*, 37.
185. Ervin, interview by author, 26 February 2007.
186. Ervin, *Conversion-Initiation and Baptism in the Holy Spirit*, 37.
187. Ervin, *These Are Not Drunken, As Ye Suppose*, 84.
188. Ervin, interview by author, 26 February 2007.
189. Ervin, *These Are Not Drunken, As Ye Suppose*, 84–85.
190. Chad Owen, ed. *Perspectives on Spirit Baptism: Five Views* (Nashville: Broadman & Holman, 2004), 118.
191. Anthony Hoekema, *Holy Spirit Baptism* (Grand Rapids: Eerdmans, 1972), 80.
192. Hoekema, 80.
193. Hoekema, 81.
194. Hoekema, 81.
195. Hoekema, 82.
196. Hoekema, 82.
197. Ervin, *Spirit Baptism*, 44.
198. Ervin, *These Are Not Drunken, As Ye Suppose*, 42.
199. Ervin, *These Are Not Drunken, As Ye Suppose*, 46.
200. Hoekema, 83.
201. Hoekema, 83.
202. Hoekema, 86.
203vHoekema, 93.
204. Dunn, *Baptism in the Holy Spirit*, 54.
205. Dunn, *Baptism in the Holy Spirit*, 96.
206. Dunn, *Baptism in the Holy Spirit*, 100.
207. Dunn, *Baptism in the Holy Spirit*, 71.
208. Dunn, *Baptism in the Holy Spirit*, 71.

209. Dunn, *Baptism in the Holy Spirit*, 71.
210. Dunn, *Baptism in the Holy Spirit*, 54.
211. Dunn, *Baptism in the Holy Spirit*, 71.
212. Dunn, *Baptism in the Holy Spirit*, 71.
213. James Dunn, *The Acts of the Apostles* (Peterborough, UK: Epworth, 1996), 52.
214. Dunn, *The Acts of the Apostles*, 58.
215. Dunn, *Baptism in the Holy Spirit*, 71.
216. Stanley Horton. *What the Bible Says About the Holy Spirit* (Springfield, MO: Gospel Publishing, 1976).
217. Horton. *What the Bible Says About the Holy Spirit*, 150.
218. Horton. *What the Bible Says About the Holy Spirit*, 150.
219. Horton. *What the Bible Says About the Holy Spirit*, 150.
220. Stanly Horton, *The Book of Acts* (Springfield, MO: Gospel Publishing, 1981), 68.
221. Horton, *What the Bible Says About the Holy Spirit*, 151.

I thank Robert W. Graves for alerting me to another Pentecostal response to Ervin in Larry W. Hurtado, "On Being Filled with the Spirit," *Paraclete* 4: 1 (Winter 1970): 29–32. I regret that I learned of this article only after this book was in publication, and I could not include it in this study.

222. Howard M. Ervin, Professor of Old Testament at Oral Roberts University, interview by author, Tulsa, OK, 6 September 2006.
223. Roger Stronstad, *The Charismatic Theology of St. Luke* (Peabody, MA: Hendrickson, 1984).
224. Stronstad, 54.
225. Stronstad, 54.
226. Stronstad, 54.
227. Stronstad, 54.
228. Stronstad, 54.
229. Max Turner, *Power From on High* (Sheffield, UK: Sheffield Press, 1996), 165.
230. Turner, 168–169.
231. Turner, 169.

232. Turner, 169.

233. Turner, 357.

234. Turner, 167.

235. Turner, 356.

236. Turner, 167.

237. Turner, 167–168.

238. Turner, 167, n. 90.

239. James Shelton, *Mighty in Word and Deed* (Eugene, OR: Wipf and Stock Publishers, 1991), 136.

240. Shelton, 145.

241. Shelton, 145.

242. Shelton, 139.

243. Archie Hui, "*Spirit-fullness* in Luke-Acts: Technical and Prophetic?" *Journal of Pentecostal Theology* 17 (October 2000): 29.

244. Hui, 29.

245. Hui, 38.

246. Hui, 38.

247. Ervin, *These Are Not Drunken, As Ye Suppose*, 14.

248. Hui, 38.

249. Ervin, *These Are Not Drunken, As Ye Suppose*, 71.

250. Larry Hart, "Spirit Baptism: A Dimensional Charismatic Perspective," in *Perspectives on Spirit Baptism: Five Views,* ed. Chad Owen Brand (Nashville: Broadman & Holman, 2004), 118.

251. Hart, 118.

252. Hart, 119.

253. Hart, 121.

254. Hart, 122.

255. Hart, 162.

256. Ervin, *These Are Not Drunken, As Ye Suppose*, 75-76.

257. Frank Macchia, *Baptized in the Spirit: A Global Pentecostal Theology* (Grand Rapids: Zondervan, 2006), 23

258. Macchia, 77.

259. Andreas J. Kostenberger, "What Does It Mean to be Filled with the Spirit" *Journal of Evangelical Theological Society* 40 (January 1997): 236.

260. Kostenberger, 237.

261. Ben Witherington III., *Acts of the Apostles: A Socio-Rhetorical Commentary* (Grand Rapids: Eerdmans, 1998), 133.

262. Witherington, 133.

263. Craig Keener, *Gift and Giver: The Holy Spirit for Today* (Grand Rapids: Baker, 2001), 159.

264. Keener, 151.

265. French L. Arrington "Indwelling, Baptism and Filling with the Holy Spirit: A Definition of Terms," *Pneuma* 3, no. 2 (Fall 1981): 7.

266. Arrington, 9.

267. Eduard Schweizer, *The Holy Spirit* (Philadelphia: Fortress Press, 1980), 75.

268. Killian McDonnell and George T. Montague *Christian Initiation and Baptism in the Holy Spirit* (Collegeville, MI: Liturgical Press, 1994), 31.

269. McDonnell and Montague, 31.

# Bibliography

## Books

Alexander, P. H. "Ervin, Howard Matthew." *Dictionary of Pentecostal and Charismatic Movements* Edited by Stanley Burgess and Gary B. McGee. Grand Rapids: Zondervan, 1988, 264.

Brand, Chad Owen, ed. *Perspectives on Spirit Baptism: Five Views.* Nashville: Broadman & Holman, 2004.

Dunn, James D. G. *The Acts of the Apostles.* Peterborough, UK: Eppworth, 1996.

_____. *Baptism in the Holy Spirit.* London UK: SCM Press, 1970.

Elbert, Paul, ed. "Editors Preface," In *Essays on Apostolic Themes: Studies in Honor of Howard M. Ervin Presented to Him by Colleagues and Friends on His Sixty-Fifth Birthday,* v-vi. Peabody, MA: Hendrickson Publishers, 1986.

Ervin, Howard M. *And Forbid Not To Speak With Tongues.* Plainfield, NJ: Logos Publishing, 1971.

_____. *Conversion-Initiation and Baptism in the Holy Spirit.* Peabody, MA: Hendrickson Publishers, 1984.

_____. *Healing: Sign of the Kingdom.* Peabody, MA: Hendrickson Publishers, 2002.

_____. *Spirit Baptism: A Biblical Investigation.* Peabody, MA: Hendrickson Publishers, 1987.

_____. *That Which You See and Hear.* Plainfield, NJ: Logos Publishing, 1972.

_____. *These Are Not Drunken, As Ye Suppose.* Plainfield, NJ: Logos Publishing, 1968.

Farrah, Charles, and Steve Durasoff. "Biographic and Bibliographical Sketch." In *Essays on Apostolic Themes: Studies in Honor of Howard M. Ervin Presented to Him by Colleagues and Friends on His Sixty-Fifth Birthday,* ed. Paul Elbert, xi–xiv. Peabody, MA: Hendrickson, 1985.

Forbes, James. "Foreword." In *Essays on Apostolic Themes: Studies in Honor of Howard M. Ervin Presented to Him by Colleagues and Friends on His Sixty-Fifth Birthday,* ed. Paul Elbert, xix. Peabody, MA: Hendrickson, 1985.

Hart, Larry. "Spirit Baptism: A Dimensional Charismatic Perspective." In *Perspectives on Spirit Baptism: Five Views,* ed. Chad Owen Brand, 105–165. Nashville: Broadman & Holman, 2004.

Harrell, Jr. David Edwin. *Oral Roberts: An American Life.* Bloomington, IN: Indiana University Press, 1985.

Hoekema, Anthony A. *Holy Spirit Baptism.* Grand Rapids: Eerdmans Publishing, 1972.

Horton, Stanley M. *The Book of Acts.* Springfield, MO: Gospel Publishing, 1981.

_____. *What the Bible Says About the Holy Spirit.* Springfield, MO: Gospel Publishing House, 1976.

Keener, Craig S. *Gift and Giver: The Holy Spirit for Today.* Grand Rapids: Baker, 2001.

Lederle, H. I. *Treasures Old and New: Interpretations of "Spirit-Baptism" in the Charismatic Renewal Movement.* Peabody, MA: Hendrickson, 1988.

Macchia, Frank. *Baptized in the Spirit: A Global Pentecostal Theology.* Grand Rapids: Zondervan, 2006.

McDonnell, Kilian, and George T. Montague. *Christian Initiation and Baptism in the Holy Spirit.* Collegeville, MI: Liturgical Press, 1994.

Menzies, William W., and Robert P. Menzies. *Spirit and Power: Foundations of Pentecostal Experience.* Grand Rapids: Zondervan, 2000.

Rae, John, ed. *The Layman's Commentary on the Holy Spirit.* Plainfield, NJ: Logos International, 1972.

Rathbun, Russell. *Post Rapture Radio.* San Francisco: Jossey-Bass. 1995.

Shelton, James B. *Mighty in Word and Deed.* Eugene, OR: Wipf and Stock Publishers, 1991.

Schweizer, Eduard. *The Holy Spirit.* Philadelphia: Fortress Press, 1980.

Stronstad, Roger *The Charismatic Theology of St. Luke*. Peabody, MA: Hendrickson Publishers, 1984.

Turner, Max. *Power from on High*. Sheffield, UK: Sheffield Press, 1996.

Witherington III., Ben. *Acts of the Apostles: A Socio-Rhetorical Commentary*. Grand Rapids: Eerdmans, 1998.

## *Periodicals*

Ervin, Howard M. "For Such A Time As This." "For Such a Time as This." *Outreach*, no. 1 (1965): 24–26.

French, Arrington L. "Indwelling, Baptism and Filling with the Holy Spirit: A Definition of Terms." *Pneuma* 3, no. 2 (Fall 1981): 1–10.

Harrup, Scott. "Practicing Pentecost." *Enrichment Journal* 10 (Winter 2005): 40.

Hui, Archie. "Spirit-fullness in Luke-Acts: Technical and Prophetic?" *Journal of Pentecostal Theology* 17 (October 2000): 24–38.

Kostenberger, Andreas J. "What Does It Mean to be Filled with the Spirit?" *Journal of Evangelical Theological Society* 40 (January 1997): 229–240.

Porter, Elizabeth. "Dr. Howard Ervin Retires after 40 Years of Teaching." *The University Oracle*, 6 December 2007. sec. A, p. 2.

Phillips, McCandlish. "And There Appeared To Them Tongues Of Fire." *Saturday Evening Post*, 16 May 1964, 31.

## *Other Sources*

Clark, Gary, Chairman of Holy Spirit Renewal Ministries in American Baptist Churches. Interview by author. Cleveland, TN. 9 March 2007. mp3 recording.

Elbert, Paul. Interview by author. Cleveland, TN. 10 February 2007. mp3 recording.

Ervin, Howard M. "Filled Continuously," Holy Spirit Research Center, Oral Roberts University, 1980. audiocassette.

_____. "John's Pneumatology." Lecture from GTHE 692

Pneumatology, Oral Roberts University. 2 February 2006. Mp3 recording by author.

_____. "Howard M. Ervin Retirement Reception." Oral Roberts University. 5 December 2006. Mp3 recording by author.

_____. Interview by Robert W. Graves, President of the Foundation for Pentecostal Scholarship. Tulsa, OK. November, 1980. audiocassette.

_____. Professor of Old Testament at Oral Roberts University. Interview by author. Tulsa, OK. 9 February 2006.

_____. Professor of Old Testament at Oral Roberts University. Interview by author. Tulsa, OK. 6 September 2006.

_____. Professor of Old Testament at Oral Roberts University. Interview by author. Tulsa, OK. 26 February 2007.

_____. Professor of Old Testament at Oral Roberts University. Interview by author. Tulsa, OK. 8 January, 2008.

_____. "My Testimony." Holy Spirit Research Center, Oral Roberts University, Tulsa, OK. 1968. audiocassette.

_____. "My Testimony," Holy Spirit Research Center, Oral Roberts University, Tulsa, OK. 3 October 1969. audiocassette.

_____. "Pilgrimage into Pentecost." Ervin Publications. Holy Spirit Research Center, Oral Roberts University, Tulsa, OK. n.d. audiocassette.

_____. "A Rationale for Tongues." First American Baptist Conference on the Holy Spirit. Holy Spirit Research Center, Oral Roberts University. 10 September 1975. audiocassette.

_____. "Testimony." Day of Renewal at St. Nicholas Catholic Charismatic Center.. Holy Spirit Research Center, Oral Roberts University, Tulsa, OK. Oct 1978. audiocassette.

Graves, Robert W., President, Foundation for Pentecostal Scholarship (rgraves@tffps.org) Reply to Query Regarding Howard M. Ervin. Email to Daniel D. Isgrigg (danny@christianchapel.com) (3 January 2007).

Graves, Robert W., "Presidents Top Ten." The Foundation for Pentecostal Scholarship. January 2007. http://www.tffps.org/top10htm. (January 2007).

Letter to Howard Ervin read by Dr. Ralph Fagin, Vice President for Academic Affairs. "Howard M. Ervin Retirement Reception." Oral Roberts University, Tulsa, OK. 5 December 2006. Mp3 recording by author.

Mathew, Thomson K., Dean of School of Theology and Missions. "Howard M. Ervin Retirement Reception." Oral Roberts University. 5 December 2006. Mp3 recording by author.

Menzies, William. (wwmenzies@mchsil.com) Reply to Query Regarding Howard M. Ervin. Email to Daniel D. Isgrigg (danny@christianchapel.com) (7 January 2007).

"One Hundredth Anniversary: 1893-1993" Atlantic Highlands, NJ: Central Baptist Church, pamphlet.

# Subject Index

American Baptist Church, 14, 28, 29
    Northern Baptist Convention of, 14
baptism in the Holy Spirit, 40-46
definition, 39, 44-46, 90, 93, 103
    evangelical view of, 34-35, 44, 48-50, 90, 98, 99-102, 104-106, 125,
terms, 44-46, 60
    of Jesus, 60
    subsequent to salvation, 26, 34, 35, 38, 43, 44, 47, 52, 56, 61, 62-68, 73,90, 98-99, 101, 106, 109, 112, 119, 124
Bennett, Dennis, 20
Bredesen, Harald, 19-20, 22
Central Baptist Church, Atlantic Highlands, NJ, 14, 18, 21, 135, 151
Charismatic(s)
Renewal, 14, 22, 24, 25, 26, 27, 74, 125
Baptist, 6, 29, 131
Roman Catholic, 26-28, 125
Clark, Gary, 29
*Conversion Initiation and the Baptism in the Holy Spirit*, 36-38, 40, 42, 104
Corvin, R. O., 23, 40
du Plessis, David, 19, 20, 22, 28, 40
Dunn, James D.G., 27, 32, 33, 35-38, 40, 63, 86, 98, 104-106
Eastern Baptist Theological Seminary (EBTS), 13-15
Elbert, Paul, 32-34, 41
Emmanuel Baptist Church, Atlantic Highlands, NJ, 14, 21-22, 23, 27, 28, 131, 135
Ervin, Howard,
    baptism in the Holy Spirit, 16-22
conversion, 11, 12
ecumenical impact, 22, 23-30, 130-131

education, 13, 23, 24, 34, 73, 135
   family, 11, 15, 18, 29
professor, 15-16, 23-25,
   works, 39-42
empowerment, 6, 26, 35, 38, 44, 52-53, 60, 67, 77, 84, 90-92, 100-103, 105-106
evidential tongues, 18-19, 26, 29, 39, 43, 53-58, 61-68, 78
First Baptist Church, Lansdale, PA, 11-14
fruit of the Spirit, 50, 57, 98, 103, 104
Full Gospel Business Men's Fellowship International (FGBMI), 19, 20, 22, 23, 25, 41, 127
Graves, Robert W., 34, 36-37
healing, 21-22, 41, 61, 69-71
   of the church, 14, 25, 28
Hoekema, Anthony, 98-104
Holy Spirit, personhood of, 54, 57, 58, 78-80
Horton, Stanley M., 98, 106-109
Hui, Archie, 116-118
Johannine pneumatology, 4, 52, 51
   new birth, 17, 47-50, 51, 60
Pentecost, 47
Kostenberger, Andreas J., 122,
Lederle, Henry I., 32
Lukan pneumatology, 31, 35, 37, 50-51, 102, 111-112
Luke-Acts, 31, 32, 33, 38, 44, 53, 92, 101, 109-110, 116, 123, 128
Macchia, Frank D., 121,
Mathew, Thomson K., 24, 32
McDonnell, Fr. Killian, 28, 125
MacNutt, (Fr.) Francis, 27
Menzies, William M., 5-6, 32
multiple fillings, *See* one baptism—one filling
Murray, Alfred L., 11-12, 13, 14
one baptism—one filling, 6, 36, 62, 73-95, 97-98, 105, 120, 126
Oral Roberts Ministry Partners Seminar, 22, 23, 25, 127
Oral Roberts University, 14, 16, 22-25, 27, 29, 36, 40, 127, 131, 133

*154*

Osteen, John, 19
Pentecost, Day of, 16-17, 19, 46, 47-52, 57, 80-82, 110
    as the birthday of the church, 5, 16, 47-52, 104, 106
Pentecostalism, 27, 32, 36, 37, 38, 40, 74, 97, 127, 130
    critiques of, 36, 99, 119
    distinctive doctrines of, 26, 32, 35, 90, 97, 109,
    scholarship, 33, 34, 38, 107, 127, 129
Roberts, Oral, 22, 23, 136
Roman Catholic-Pentecostal Dialogues, 28
Princeton Theological Seminary, 13, 19, 29, 34, 73
salvation, 48-50, 52, 63, 67, 68, 73, 91-92
Septuagint, 13, 109, 114
Shelton, James B., 34, 109, 115-116
Society for Pentecostal Studies, 36, 41, 42, 128, 133
Spirit baptism, *See* baptism in the Holy Spirit
spiritual gifts, *charisms,* 34, 39, 41, 57, 69-71
Stronstad, Roger, 34, 98, 109-112, 122
*These Are Not Drunken, As Ye Suppose,* 15, 32, 35, 39, 40, 128
Tyson, Tommy, 19

# Scripture Index

**GENESIS**
- 1-2        17
- 2:7        17

**LUKE**
- 3:16       44, 104
- 4:1        60, 85, 113
- 4:14       60
- 12:12      83
- 24:45-53   62

**JOHN**
- 3:5-8      50
- 15:4       50
- 17         28
- 20:19-23   17, 23, 47, 49
- 20:28      49

**ACTS**
- 1:5        44, 76, 104
- 1:8        44, 53, 83
- 2:4        17, 44, 46, 54, 62, 76, 80, 90, 101, 106, 110, 112, 114, 122, 126
- 2:17       54
- 2:33       48
- 2:39       66
- 3:6-7      83
- 4:8        38, 82-83, 85-89, 106, 108, 110, 112, 114, 115, 122, 126
- 4:31       36, 38, 42, 62, 81, 82, 85-89, 106, 110, 112, 114, 122, 126
- 8:14-17    63
- 8:38-39    84
- 9:7        65
- 10:44      46, 6-67
- 11:15-17   44, 46, 104

*13:9*     38
*13:52*    107, 110

**ROMANS**
*10:9-10*    48, 50
*12*         70

**1 CORINTHIANS**
*12*        69
*12:13*    52, 102
*14:15*    56

**GALATIANS**
*5:16-25*    50

**EPHESIANS**
*4*          70
*5:18*     77, 103, 120, 123

**2 JOHN**
*1*          15

www.ingramcontent.com/pod-product-compliance
Ingram Content Group UK Ltd.
Pitfield, Milton Keynes, MK11 3LW, UK
UKHW041448180426
11946UKWH00001B/3